THE MISSIONARY'S WIFE

THE MISSIONARY'S WIFE

A MEMOIR OF MRS.

M. A. HENDERSON

OF DEMERARA

BY

THOMAS HENDERSON

SEVENTEEN YEARS A MISSIONARY
IN BRITISH GUIANA

"MY HELPER IN CHRIST JESUS."—PAUL.

CURIOSMITH

MINNEAPOLIS

Published by Curiosmith.
Minneapolis, Minnesota.
Internet: curiosmith.com.

The text of this edition is from *The Missionary's Wife: A Memoir of Mrs. M. A. Henderson of Demerara*, by her husband, seventeen years a missionary in British Guiana. London: John Snow, 1855.

ISBN 9781946145666

CONTENTS

CONTENTS *(Continued)*

TO

SUNDAY SCHOOL TEACHERS

IN GREAT BRITAIN AND THE MISSION FIELD,

𝔗𝔥𝔦𝔰 𝔞𝔱𝔱𝔢𝔪𝔭𝔱

TO RECORD THE LABORS OF ONE WHO

CONSECRATED HER LIFE

TO THE SERVICE OF THE SAVIOUR,

IS,

WITH EARNEST PRAYER THAT IT MAY ADVANCE

THE INTERESTS OF SUNDAY SCHOOLS,

RESPECTFULLY INSCRIBED,

BY THEIR FELLOW LABORER,

THE AUTHOR.

PREFACE

The history of this Volume is soon told. While preparing a sketch of the character and employments of my deceased wife, who was so valuable an instructor, the matter accumulated beyond the proportions usually allotted in periodical literature. But, assured of the value of her example as a teacher, and the interest which her biography might excite in youthful minds, such as those by whom she had been fondly esteemed, I was led to contemplate the preparation of a more extended Memoir. This, however, was not undertaken without some misgivings of my inability to accomplish the design with satisfaction to myself. The limited materials I had at command, and other disadvantages under which the work must be prosecuted, made me hesitate. I earnestly solicit for the ensuing pages the exercise of Christian charity and forbearance, and trust those individuals who may be induced to peruse the Volume will judge kindly of the production.

The Work is designed, under the divine blessing, to excite a greater interest in Sunday Schools; to encourage any who may have to pass through similar mental conflicts; and contribute in some measure to edify the people of God, and stimulate the friends of Missions.

The course described in these pages is comparatively short. Of the subject of them it may be said, her "sun went down while it was yet noon." It is the devout desire of the compiler that those illustrations of divine grace may serve to extend the Redeemer's kingdom and manifest the constraining power of his love in the hearts of his people.

THOMAS HENDERSON.
LONDON, *February*, 1855.

CHAPTER 1

Birth—Early Years—Enters Kent Street Sunday School—Miss N———'s Letter—Bible Class Exercises—Letter to Negro Girl—Questions to Teacher—Strong Convictions—Becomes Decided—Enters Borough Road School.

In recording these incidents in the life of Mrs. HENDERSON, the Writer will not detain the reader with an ancestral list of great names; though he need not be ashamed of those whose reputation depends only on moral worth. The subject of this memoir might have claimed relationship to a family of illustrious Nonconformists, who bore the name of her maternal parent.

Mary Anne, the eldest daughter of Robert and Mary Leslie, was born in London, on the tenth day of January, 1820. Although her parents made no decided profession of religion when their daughter was a child, yet it was the anxious desire of each that their children should be nurtured in the fear of the Lord. This was particularly manifested by her excellent mother, who was considered to have been "a disciple secretly" for years before her public profession of faith in Christ. From childhood Mary Anne was affectionate and tender-hearted, and devotedly attached to her parents. She possessed warmth of heart and an ingenuous temperament, which bound her closely to all who shared in her affection and love. Referring to this period, after she became a mother, she said, "In childhood, a reproof, even *implied*, by my mother, would break my heart; but to censure, from persons whom I did not love, I could be perfectly indifferent." In early childhood, she could read, and was ever extremely fond of books. Her memory was early stored with hymns, chapters of the Bible, and religious facts; but, although naturally susceptible of impressions, years passed before they produced really beneficial and lasting effect upon her mind.

When ten years old, she was the subject of frequent and strong convictions. At such times she would resolve to give her heart to God. Ultimately, having broken so many, she began to think it hopeless to make any more resolutions. Still, she did not and could not give up the thought of being one day a child of God.

In 1831 her parents removed to the Dover Road, when Mary Anne and her sisters were placed at the Kent Street Sunday School—a nursery where many renewed souls have been trained for usefulness, and become ornaments of the Church of God. She was of an amiable disposition, and delighted in pleasing her kind teachers, from whose lips she heard of the Saviour's love—which brought her, soon after, as a willing captive to the foot of the cross.

The writer of the following letter, being fully competent to form a just estimate of her character and talents, has kindly supplied some facts in this part of her life.

"At your request, dear Sir, I will try to remember a few incidents in the early days of your deceased wife and my beloved Sunday scholar, by whose removal the Church and the world suffer no common loss. Hers was no *ordinary* career. How mysterious, that it should end so soon! We must bow with submission, and learn to say, 'Thy will be done.'

"Mary Anne had been in Kent Street Sunday School a year or two before she was placed in the Bible class. She was then twelve years of age, and astonished and interested me with her mental powers. She spared no pains or trouble. On one occasion, all the class had to learn passages of Scripture upon one of the attributes of God. Each class had to commit to memory different passages, on

the several attributes. Mary Anne was not contented with the portion assigned her, but she gathered from the whole of the classes the
entire selections, wrote every verse out in full (making quite a little
volume), and modestly said, when she handed them to me, 'It was
to save you the trouble of turning to each passage.' At the end, each
verse was turned into metre, almost in Scripture words. On asking
her, some years after, if these verses were preserved, she said, 'No.'
This is matter of regret, as they displayed much ingenuity and talent in such a child. Indeed, none ever knew of their existence but
myself.

"A little circumstance occurs to me, connected with the West
Indies, which I may mention, as it perhaps tended in some degree to
foster in Mary Anne a Missionary spirit. The Rev. J. Houghton and
his family, from Surrey Chapel, were about to embark for Jamaica,
in the Missionary work. He came one afternoon to Kent Street and
addressed the school. At its close the Bible classes expressed a wish
to make some little presents, and send some Testaments and letters. Mr. Houghton kindly consented to take charge of anything
entrusted to his care. Accordingly, these girls met their teachers once
or twice a week, in the Schoolroom, until a number of articles of
various descriptions were completed, including clothing, etc. There
were, I think, fifty large Testaments, each in a separate bag, with a
note from the girl who sent them, to one of her own age in Jamaica.
Having preserved a few of these notes, I will transcribe Mary Anne's.

"'TO A GIRL OF MY OWN AGE—FOURTEEN YEARS.

"'My dear little Friend—I am very pleased to write you a few
lines and send it with a Testament, which I hope you will be able
to read, and that it will do you good. I hope you will soon have
kind teachers, as we have, who will teach you the way to heaven.
We, in England, enjoy a great many advantages. There are a great
many chapels and schools: ours is a very large one. We have between
500 and 600 children, and more than 40 teachers. It is called Kent

Street Sunday School. I should be very glad to receive a letter from you. We often talk of children abroad. I should like to see you very much; but, if we do not meet on earth, if we love and come to Jesus Christ we shall all be together in heaven. I send you this with my love.

"'Your affectionate friend,

"'M. A. Leslie.'

"Mr. Houghton and his family, soon after embarking, were shipwrecked off the English coast, and barely escaped with their lives. They were obliged to return to London, while the ship was being repaired, to obtain a fresh outfit. Everything on board was lost, except this box, which, after the vessel was deserted by passengers, was found floating upon a piece of the wreck. This preservation was thought remarkable. Again, with the Missionary, it was put on board, and reached its destination just in time for the contents to be presented to the negro children on the memorable first of August, 1834. Mr. Houghton, in a letter to a teacher soon after, stated how much those little presents had contributed to the pleasure of that happy day.

"Her aptness in finding proofs, while reading in the Bible class, was manifest, and generally correct. She very readily detected any mistake in quoting Scripture. Her lessons were repeated correctly, and with unusual seriousness. She sometimes put questions which indicated attention to what passed at the desk. One Sabbath she inquired if Mr. —— was right when he said in prayer—'Grant, O Lord, that many, yea, all, these children, *if it be thy will*, may be saved. May they bring forth fruit—some thirty, some fifty, and some an hundred-fold, to thy glory.' 'Now, teacher,' she asked, 'is it *not* the will of God that *all* should be saved?' I replied, 'To the law and the testimony, Mary Anne. What does the Bible say about it?' With her accustomed tact, she said, 'I think these do'—'It is *not* the will of your heavenly Father that one of these little ones should perish.' 'God willeth *not* the death of a sinner,' 'This is the will of God, even your sanctification.' 'Why,' she said, 'ask for thirtyfold, when we may have an *hundredfold?*'

"At this period, and as long as she remained at home, it was her custom to take her three younger sisters, every Sabbath, upstairs, to hear them repeat their afternoon lessons, and then kneel down and pray with them. She tried also to supply the want of family prayer, by reading, morning and evening, the Scriptures in her father's house; and as soon as she was able, she paid for a pew in Union Street Chapel, for the accommodation of her parents and sisters."

On Easter Tuesday, 1833, Mr. Crabbe, one of the teachers at Kent Street, addressed a kind and seasonable letter to the young scholar, urging upon her *"the importance of early decision for God."* This letter came most opportunely, for on the previous Friday Mary Anne heard a sermon which was preached to the Sunday Schools in Bermondsey, from the words "I love them that love me, and those who seek me early shall find me." On the following Lord's-day Mr. R. N—— addressed the school, from the Saviour's words to Peter— "Lovest thou me?" "On each of these occasions," Mary Anne wrote, in a memorandum of her feelings, "my conscience was aroused, and I resolved to be able to answer the question affirmatively before the next week; but I should probably have soon forgot, and not remembered it again, or at least for a considerable time, had not Mr. Crabbe's letter been, about the same time, put into my hand. The perusal of this letter awakened powerful convictions of sin. I no longer felt that a future time would do, but my mind was agonized with the belief that I had sinned away the day of grace—that now, for me, nothing was reserved but the blackness of darkness for ever. Affectionate admonitions, fervent prayers, offered by my teachers, and broken vows, now all crowded into my mind; and for days and weeks nothing but despair seized upon me. It was at this time my custom to lock myself in my bedroom, and, spreading the letter on my bed, kneel down and earnestly implore God to save me. I felt that God would be *just* were he to banish me for ever from his presence; but 'who shall dwell with everlasting burnings?' was my constant question. So overwhelming were my feelings at this time, that I more than once meditated self destruction, and once walked to the steps of Blackfriars Bridge for the purpose of putting an end to my existence; but the knowledge that 'no murderer hath eternal life abiding in him' stopped me. I felt that while God granted life, there was hope; but that in destroying life I must be the murderer of my own soul. For a long time I did not unfold my state of mind to anyone, and studiously concealed my feelings. My dear mother, however, was too observant not to notice that a great change had passed over me. This, no doubt, was manifested in ways which I did not think of. She did not make any remark, but, some time after, inquired what led me to my own room so much, morning and evening; and, when finding her suspicions correct, requested me to take my sisters with me sometimes.[1]

"After several weeks spent in the gloom of despair, I was at length, through the mercy of God, brought to trust simply to Jesus for salvation, and thus found peace. Some time after, Mr. Crabbe again wrote to me, and requested me to answer his letter. This led to a series of most interesting letters from him; and the exercise of replying was productive of much profit to me. Great was his joy when he found he had been instrumental in bringing my soul to Christ.

"Also at this time, my mother attended the ministry of the late Rev. John Arundel, Union Street, Southwark; I accompanied her in the morning, and in the evening attended a Bible class conducted by a devoted member of Mr. Arundel's Church. She frequently urged upon me the duty of uniting myself with the Church. Though I had never avowed to her the change which had taken place, she hoped the best."

---

1 Such was the intensity of her feelings at this time, and her earnest desire to become a child of God, that she copied Doddridge's form of covenant, and signed it with her own blood.

Of the valuable instructions communicated in that interesting Bible class, and also in Kent Street School, both conducted by excellent and honored teachers, the subject of this memoir always spoke gratefully, and cherished affectionate remembrance of the instructors.

Believing that she was intended, by Him who had endowed her with capacities and powers, for usefulness, Miss N—— proposed to her parents that Mary Anne should enter the British and Foreign School Society's Central School, with the view of ultimately being trained for a teacher. This proposal proved to be in harmony with her ardent mind. From the time of her entering the Borough Road School she made encouraging progress, and the committee and superintendent consulted how they might retain so promising a pupil. Though before the age stated in the rules, they raised her to a paid monitor's rank, and afterwards received her into the institution altogether.

Upwards of nine years and a half the subject of this memoir remained in that valuable institution, in the capacity of a pupil teacher, teacher, and assistant superintendent; and during the whole of these years uniformly received from Mrs. MacRae, the indefatigable superintendent, and from the ladies of the committee, the greatest kindnesses.

"When, at the early age of fifteen, the superintendent of Kent Street School had appointed her to take charge of a class, she wrote me a note expressing her deep sense of unfitness, and that nothing but a sense of duty, and receiving it as a call from God to work for him, could make her willing to undertake it. She was soon valued as one of the most efficient among us."[1]

---

1 Miss N——'s letter to the Writer, by whom much information has been kindly furnished.

CHAPTER 2

Joins the Church at Union Street, Southwark—Forms Studious Habits—Mrs. MacRae's Letter—Mother's Death—Desires Missionary Work—Interview with Miss N.—Farewell Meeting at her Pastor's House.

In the early part of the following year (1835), the young teacher's mind became deeply impressed with the obligation of making a public profession of Christ, which was strengthened by frequent conversations with an endeared young friend, whose acquaintance she had formed at the Borough Road. This led to an interview with her esteemed minister, to whom she addressed the following letter:—

"Having first sought direction from on high, I will attempt to communicate a few of my thoughts with regard to joining a Christian Church. It has long been urged upon my serious consideration; but my unbelieving heart was always ready to find obstacles numerous and insurmountable—such as my being too young, too guilty, and altogether unfit for such a privilege. Not that these doubts and fears have been entirely banished from my mind; but I endeavor to look out of myself to Him who has promised to give strength for the performance of every duty.

"I was, I trust, brought to a saving knowledge of Christ through the medium of a letter addressed to me by one of our Sabbath School teachers, who attended our writing class, and had not been known to me more than a month. I had before received many impressions, and had often been affectionately urged to come to the Saviour; but, alas! these had proved ineffectual. I had from time to time resolved that, let others do as they would, I would serve the Lord; but this resolution was made in my own strength, and entirely failed till the divine Spirit was pleased, of his abundant mercy, to open my eyes to see my true condition in the presence of a holy God.

"That a comparative stranger should manifest so great an anxiety for the welfare of my immortal soul, while I was totally unconcerned about it, produced deep and lasting impressions upon my mind, which had, I trust, led to an entire dependence on the Saviour. This took place in the beginning of May, 1832. I have since found Christ to be all in all, and desire henceforth to live to his glory, who has called me out of darkness into his marvellous light. I would now come forward, and

'—— tell to all around
What a dear Saviour I have found.'

"I am, Sir, yours, etc.,
"MARY ANNE LESLIE."

She was received on the 13th September, 1835, into the fellowship of the Congregational Church assembling in Union Street, Southwark, under the pastoral care of the late Rev. John Arundel. On this occasion both the ladies who conducted the Bible classes at Union Street and Kent Street were present. The union formed that day between the pastor and the youthful member was characterized by strong and unabated affection in after years, and resulted in blessed effects. In life, both were mutually attached; and "in death they were not" *long* "divided." Where they now are united, there is but "one Shepherd and one sheepfold."

Feeling that the Church to which she had deliberately united herself now demanded all her energies, Mary Anne left Kent Street Sunday School for Union Street School. Those who knew her best can tell that, whatever she undertook, *she did with all her might;* she did nothing by halves: and in nothing was this more seen than in the work of instruction. Although by far the junior of her coadjutors, it was not long before she was appointed superintendent, and afterwards secretary, of the Sunday School, both which offices she held until her departure for the West Indies. The Christian Instruction and Missionary Societies connected with the congregation had also a share of her time and labor. In company with her pastor's younger daughter, she visited for several years a district in the Borough where they had to encounter difficulties and witness scenes which would have shaken stronger nerves; but, womanlike, these two young females courageously persevered in their "work of faith and labor of love." Among the many zealous friends of Missions in Union Street Meeting, few outdid Mary Anne in steady continuous efforts for the advancement of the Redeemer's kingdom. The Ragged Schools had also a share of her time and sympathy.

From the time of her entering the training institution of the British and Foreign School Society, she became an assiduous student, and resolved to excel in everything she had to learn and teach. In addition to the everyday labor in the Central School, evening classes, etc., she devoted hours which should have been given to sleep in devouring the contents of numerous works; and even before the hour of teaching returned, she might have been found pacing the floor of the schoolroom, solving problems in Euclid, and acquiring a knowledge of Latin and French. Hence it was that Mary Anne became so efficient in the art of teaching.

Few of the many advantages which London affords were neglected by her, but she found none more useful than the excellent female Bible class conducted for so many years by that able expositor of divine truth, the Rev. John Campbell, D.D. For successive years it was her privilege to receive from his lips instructions which eminently qualified her in after life for expounding the sacred volume, and made her a clear, interesting, and successful teacher of its doctrines. Through all weathers did she walk from the Borough Road to the Tabernacle, Moorfields; nor could she be prevailed upon to desist in the dark and stormy nights of winter. Such was her thirst for knowledge, that she would have encountered any amount of labor to add to her stock. Her attention and progress, her attainments and influence among her associates, gave her a place in the esteem and affection of her honored instructor, which, after many years, he has been prompt to remember. The gratitude of those who profited by her attainments, and were benefited by her matured counsels, are due to him who labored to expand her mind and prepare her and others for usefulness.

As an evidence of the assiduity with which she studied her Bible, the following incident may be adduced:—In the second edition of the "Bible with 20,000 emendations," now published by C. N. Bartlett, the observant reader may perceive a new rendering of Exodus 34:7, as compared with the previous edition. It was the subject of this memoir who directed the attention of the Editor to the error which occurred in the previous rendering of that passage.

A deep sense of the great benefits which she derived from attendance on the valuable instructions received at the Tabernacle class, led her afterwards to take a great interest in Bible classes, and do all she could to establish and encourage them.

Of Mary Anne's diligence and labors during the time she resided in the Model School, Borough Road, the following testimony is borne by one who witnessed every day her zeal in the work of instruction, and the delight she felt in teaching: to her it was a "labor of love."

"My dear Sir—In answer to your inquiries respecting my late much loved friend, Mrs. Henderson, I regret that my numerous engagements prevent my entering so fully into your wishes as seems desirable; still I have great pleasure in bearing testimony to her valuable services during the time she was a teacher in our Model School. She was first introduced to me by Miss Newsom, as a very promising girl, whose whole train of thought and character had given most satisfactory and pleasing evidences of early piety. On this she was admitted as a pupil, and soon made such rapid progress in various branches of instruction that she was appointed to the charge of a class, which afforded an opportunity for the exercise and development of those qualifications for which, as a public teacher, she ultimately became so eminent. After some years' diligent application to her studies in the Model School, she was strongly recommended to the committee as in every way qualified to fill a vacancy that then occurred for an assistant teacher. This she was successful in obtaining; and, in addition to the duties which now devolved upon her, she continued unremitting in her attention to her own studies, frequently rising at four and five o'clock in the morning to pursue a course of reading, or to master some difficulties in preparing lessons. Her Bible was her constant companion—her mind was stored with Scripture truths; and being gifted with a very retentive memory, she could with all the earnestness of a Christian teacher bring them to bear most profitably on the mind and religious training of her pupils.

"She had a great love for Missionary work, and often expressed a strong desire that she might be some day employed in heathen lands; and with this view she lost no opportunity of acquiring all that useful knowledge on common things which adapts itself to all places and all circumstances. Needlework she never liked, and therefore never excelled in it. I now set this before her as an imperative duty, and as such she diligently applied herself to it; and soon acquired such a good general knowledge of this useful art, that she frequently after referred to it, in her letters, as an invaluable accomplishment to a Missionary's wife. As a teacher she worked earnestly and prayerfully; and while her chief aim was to inculcate the great truths of the gospel, her own practice and conversation showed that she was acting under the constraining influence of redeeming love.

I believe her labors were blessed to many; while she herself was permitted to partake of a share of that blessedness which the learned cannot acquire by dint of knowledge, nor shall the simple miss for want of capacity.

"But her work is now done, and she is gone, while you are left, and all her little ones, deeply to deplore her loss. Still, are you not comforted in your silent sorrowings by a still small voice whispering, 'Blessed are the dead who die in the Lord'?

"With much sympathy, believe me to remain,

"My dear Sir,

"Yours very sincerely,

"Anne Eliza MacRae.

"Normal College, 30th October, 1854."

Her health having failed in 1839, several friends recommended a change of air and scene to the country. She consequently visited, during this and the following year, Harlow, Barnet, Shirly, High Wycombe, Henley, Reading, etc., where she met with many excellent Christian friends, and received much real kindnesses.

To a heart like hers, formed for friendship, the loss of those to whom she was tenderly and affectionately attached was no ordinary trial. About this time she sustained a severe trial by the removal of her first and most endeared friend—a friendship formed by love to the Saviour in each, and strengthened by deeply interesting correspondence, had united their hearts in mutual endearment.

While spending part of the summer of 1842 at Barnet, Mary Anne was unexpectedly summoned to attend the deathbed of her beloved mother. She found her suffering great agony of body; but her mind was "stayed, trusting in God." After watching the dying saint during the night, the sorrowing daughter witnessed her dear parent fall asleep in Jesus on the morning of July 15. This was the first domestic bereavement she had sustained, and the first time she realized death. Mary Anne now found herself called to supply the place of her mother to her four younger sisters; and it was then that her thorough unselfishness was seen, in her efforts to mitigate their grief, and minister to their comfort and happiness. The affectionate and devoted daughter proved a loving, tender, and faithful sister.

From the severe trial through which she had but recently passed, her health gave way again, and she availed herself of an invitation to Kettering; she was introduced to kind Christian society in that town, which is associated with so much that is interesting to the friends of the Redeemer.

From the commencement of that change of heart which led to her fellowship with the Saviour's people, it was the ardent desire of Mary Anne's soul to serve God among the heathen. Opportunities of entering the Mission field presented themselves more than once, but were declined. So early as the year 1838 she received overtures to accompany a Missionary to India, but could not see that to be the path of duty. In the summer of 1843 the Writer commenced a correspondence with her, which, after much deliberation, counsel, and prayer, terminated in her deciding to become his wife, and fellow laborer in his work in Guiana. The following account of an interview with her esteemed friend, at that time, has been kindly furnished by Miss N——:

"I shall not soon forget my feelings when my dear friend first intimated to me her thought of engaging in Missionary work. It was in a note requesting to see me at the Borough Road; breathing earnest desires to be directed, and expressive of her unworthiness to be employed in such a work, yet cherishing the hope that, if God did call her to engage in it, he would qualify her for it. She only desired to ascertain what *He* would have her to do. We spent that evening together in conversation and prayer. She told me she had consulted her dear pastor, and the Rev. J. J. Freeman, who had lately visited the colony of British Guiana, and knew the sphere of labor, who approved and encouraged her going. She felt that the ties which bound her to home could not be easily broken; yet she knew she was 'not her own,' and where God appointed she must go. In a few weeks it was decided that she should leave England to join the Demerara Mission; and when for the last time we met and prayed, side by side, how fervently did she pour out her petitions, humble and fervent, from a spirit deeply impressed with the solemn reality of her position!"

It has long been the custom of Miss N—— to devote every Friday evening to pray for those formerly under her instruction, but now occupying spheres of labor in different parts of the world; and the knowledge of this fact frequently comforted and cheered her friend and fellow laborer, while prosecuting her work in weakness among the children of Ham in British Guiana.

On tendering her resignation to the Committee of the British and Foreign School Society, she received much kindness from those ladies personally, and several valuable memorials of their love and esteem, as well as from other dear friends connected with that institution. Prior to embarking, her beloved pastor invited a select party of friends to meet his young friend at his own house, when he presented her with a beautiful copy of "Henry's Commentary"—a gift of the pastor and deacons of the Church in Union Street, Southwark, with which she had been in sacred fellowship for more than eight years.

CHAPTER 3

Embarks for Demerara—Sabbath at Sea—Absent Friends—
Arrival in George Town—Marriage—First Sabbath of Missionary
Labor—Teacher's Class—Temperance Meeting—Singular Names.

I n company with the Rev. Samuel Heywood and Mrs. Heywood,
with Miss W——, who proved a most cheerful and pleasant
companion, Mary Anne embarked on board the *Cleopatra*, for
Demerara, on Thursday, the 2nd November, 1843. A few extracts
from her journal, written expressly for her father's and sisters' use,
are here inserted.

"*Sunday, 5th.*—About noon, the captain, his wife, and all the
passengers, with some of the crew, met in the cabin; when, after
singing a Scotch version of a Psalm, Mr. Heywood read the 103rd
Psalm, and offered prayer. The rest of the day was spent in reading
on deck, or singing. Among other hymns, we sang 'Blest be the tie
that binds,' to the tune 'Reuben,' and spoke of the time and place
when last we joined in it. Thought much of the dear people at Union
Street, with their beloved pastor, and comforted ourselves with the
thought that we should be remembered in the great congregation."

"*Saturday, 18th.*—I begin to wish very much to see some of my
little English pets. I wish H. M—— were here, asking 'a thousand
and one' questions about the ship, etc.; and dear M——; and as to

little Mary Anne, she should chatter from morning to night, and from night to morning again. I dream of home every night, but find myself in my berth every morning."

"*Saturday, 25th.*—Had I been in England, it is not improbable I should have been spending the day with dear Mrs. M——, and dandling her little 'unknown.' I did not think, when there this day four weeks, it would be the last time I should see my beloved friend; but, though on the wide Atlantic, my vagrant thoughts ever and anon visit the various spots where memory loves to linger. Dear Lizzy will be glad to know that I am much pleased with 'Bridges on the 119 Psalm.' I am sure to think of her every time I read it, which is usually twice a day."

"*Sunday, 3rd December.*—Thought of those who, 'sitting around our Father's board,' would be raising a tuneful voice, and thinking of us upon the main. It is to be hoped that this temporary deprivation of Sabbath privileges will enhance their value when we are again permitted to enjoy them."

"*Monday, 11th December.*—Little Jane's birthday. I thought much and often of her yesterday, and not less today. Would that I could impress a kiss of love upon her cheek, as well as send up a fervent prayer on her behalf. My anxious wish for her is, that as she is growing in years she may advance not only in useful knowledge, but be truly a child of God. A mother's prayers are registered in heaven, and a sister's will constantly ascend from a distant land. May she be blessed and made a blessing."

The *Cleopatra* arrived in Demerara on the 13th of December, where Mary Anne was cordially welcomed and hospitably entertained by her friends the Rev. E. A. Wallbridge and Mrs. Wallbridge, the latter of whom, from that day to the hour of her friend's decease, uniformly acted the part of a mother to the stranger in a strange land. Mrs. Wallbridge was the *first* sister she met with in Guiana, and the *last* to whom she spoke, nine years and a half afterwards, when affectionately and tenderly waiting upon her dying friend.

On the 14th of December, 1843, it was the happiness of the

Writer of these memorials to be united in marriage to her who became indeed *"a helpmeet"*; a faithful wife; an intelligent, cheerful, and pleasant companion; and a zealous coadjutor in the Lord's vineyard, as well as a devoted mother to those of his now doubly bereaved children. Mrs. Henderson entered at once with prayerful earnestness upon her labors among the old and young in her husband's congregation.

The following extracts from her journal and correspondence will convey some idea of her first labors in Guiana:—

"Off Demerara.—I cannot tell you how much kindness I have experienced from Mr. and Mrs. Heywood: they have been like parents to myself and Miss W——. Indeed, we shall all part from one another with regret. Miss W—— has been truly kind and amiable. Unbroken harmony has crowned our days. Help me, my dear father and sisters, to erect an Ebenezer of praise to the Father of all our mercies. The thought that you at home, and our dear friends at Union Street, were praying for us, often cheered our hearts. Continue to seek that the blessing of God may be granted to me in my prospective labors; that I may be, under him, a light in the land on which I expect so soon to set my foot."

"December 15th.—About one o'clock on Wednesday we cast anchor. About two, Mr. Wallbridge came on board. He took us in his gig to his house. About five, Mr. Henderson arrived; and yesterday morning, at twelve, Mr. Wallbridge performed the anticipated ceremony. We left George Town soon after, and arrived at *home.* The children of the first Mrs. H. are quite at ease with me, and I feel nothing to regret in leaving England. The Wallbridges are really excellent people, and have an interesting little family."

"Sabbath, 24th.—Accompanied my dear husband to the Sabbath School; took a class partly of children and partly of adult females. I could not help fearing that the people would not understand me; but am very thankful my worst fears were disappointed. Teaching was resumed immediately after the service, as the people

live too far off to allow of their going home and returning. Took a class of female members of the Church, to teach them the first lessons of reading. Oh, could you have seen their eager looks, you would have rejoiced that I had left country and kindred to contribute to their instruction! I made use of all the negro phrases I had picked up, and was pleased to find that they quite understood me. In the evening Mr. H. went to Buxton to preach, while I assembled the domestics for reading and catechetical exercises. This is the first day of Missionary labor."

To Miss A——.
"January 1, 1844.
"How I wished that you could have witnessed the almost overwhelming scene that presented itself on the first Sabbath after my arrival here! Mr. Waddington (who, with his wife, sister, and Mrs. Heywood, were staying with us) had been preaching for Mr. H. Immediately after the service, almost the whole congregation crowded into the house to see *Missee*, and 'wish her and Massa joy.' So many strangers being present, it was amusing to see the whispering among themselves as to which was their *own Missee;* and when some who had seen me the day before gave the desired information, they immediately vociferated *'This a' we Missee'* etc.; while some of the old women literally took me up in their arms and attempted to bear me in triumph across the room; while others went upon their knees, holding my hand, and ejaculated their thanks to God who had sent some one to teach them. Scarcely a day has passed since on which one, and sometimes several, have brought their presents of fowl, duck, yam, sweet potato, oranges, cocoa nuts, mangoes, etc.; and this morning they have been paying the usual 'new year's compliment.' If simplicity and gratitude were the sum total of Christian excellencies, these people would be perfect. But there is much, very much, to do. The effects of the accursed, debasing system of slavery are to be seen everywhere, and appear so completely indigenous, that it will, I fear, be a long time ere their traces are removed from the land.

"Yesterday afternoon I took a class of the teachers, composed of deacons, fathers, and grandfathers—a formidable array, you will say; and really I thought it so, for I never felt more nervous in the contemplation of any engagement; but I found the promise hold good abundantly, 'my strength shall be made perfect in weakness.' The Church is divided into classes, all of which Mr. H. has been accustomed to meet himself. Henceforth, the females will be consigned to me; and this evening I meet the first class for the first time. O my dear friend, may I still reckon upon your prayers, that God may make me faithful and useful! The cheering assurance that we were remembered at the throne of grace, caused our hearts to rejoice; we indeed thanked God and took courage. I think I may say, that on no occasion, when we bend the suppliant knee, are our beloved friends in England, especially our Christian friends, forgotten.

"I suppose I must tell you something about my beloved husband. All may be summed up by saying, *my most sanguine expectations* are more than realized. As a Missionary, he is instant in season and out of season. Every day has its own work; and so large a share, that I really do sometimes tremble—especially on Sabbath, when he labors without cessation from morning to night. Of his duties connected with the Sabbath School I hope soon to be able to relieve him, at least in part. . . . And what message shall I send to my own beloved pastor—for I shall always call him so? My kindest love, my most grateful remembrance. I am delighted to hear that he is well. We were wishing he were here the other evening; this climate would just suit him. . . . Kind remembrance to all the dear friends whom time would fail me to attempt to name, but who are frequently and distinctly remembered. To the Sunday School teachers my kind love. . . . The late Mrs. Henderson's tomb is just behind the house; and every time I look at it I think of Mr. Waddington's prayer, and try to realize that I have been *baptized for the dead.*'"

"*Monday, 27th.*—In the afternoon the deacons and teachers took tea with us, prior to a temperance meeting which was held in the chapel in the evening. I am sure Miss S—— would have been

enraptured to have seen me assisting my zealous husband in regis-
tering names—or, as he called it, 'administering the pledge'—and
distributing some of the teetotal tracts which she gave me for this
locality. Almost everyone present signed the pledge who had not
done so previously. I have hitherto adhered to my determination to
take nothing but water in this country; and certainly I am quite as
well as when I was in England. Rum has done immense mischief
among the people, and I believe nothing but 'total abstinence' will
meet the evil. All present seemed to enjoy the meeting very much.
I could only be pleased with the sight of their happy countenances,
because most of what was said by the speakers was unintelligible to
me."

"*Sabbath*, 31*st*.—And has the last day of the year really come!
. . . In the afternoon I took the teachers, for scriptural instruction.
This class is composed of young men, of fathers, and grandfathers,
as well as all the deacons of the Church. Their willingness to receive
instruction is indeed truly gratifying. I wish you could have seen me
in what my dear husband calls 'the professor's chair.' You must not
be surprised if you hear of my going into the pulpit next!"

"*Tuesday, 2nd January*, 1844.—We have just engaged a lad to
attend to the horse, etc., named 'Goodluck.' You cannot conceive
the odd names that many of the people have here, as first names.
These were given to them in the time of slavery, by the planters. The
second names have been taken since emancipation; and frequently
there is such incongruity between the two that one's risible faculties
are strongly excited. Last night I was looking for a communion ticket
for a Mrs. J———, for a long time in vain, when I bethought myself
of asking the first name; and what should it be but Queen! and sure
enough, in looking among the Q's, I found 'Queen J———.' Indeed,
we have an abundance of kings, queens, princes, and duchesses. We
have also a great many classical names—as Cicero, Cato, Hercules,
etc.; and a few English and Scotch. The other day, while dining,
we heard a noise, when Mr. H. got up and called to '*MacRae*' to
be quiet. This almost electrified me, and I at once declared that the

boy must be my *protégé;* but I find there is a whole family of them!"

The following extract will give the English reader an idea of the wretched state of the villages in Guiana, when inundated by a heavy fall of rain:—

. . . "At the latter place (Buxton) the water is knee deep; the people are literally living in the water. Many of them have to sit upon their beds with a coal pot beside them to cook their plantains. The provision grounds are also inundated, and it is to be feared that nearly all the vegetables will rot, and that a consequent scarcity will be felt. The other day, when Mr. H. visited Buxton, he sailed in a battan (a kind of boat) from house to house; but his everyday lot is to wade, so that he is often wet through for hours together."

CHAPTER 4

Demerara Mission—Labors of Wray and Smith—Revival of the East Coast Mission—A. Simpson, Esq.—Bethel Chapel removed—First Service—New Station—New Bethel Chapel—Churches and Schools in Guiana—Government Inspector's Report.

Few fields of Mission labor possess more interest in their associations, or have yielded a more abundant harvest, than the Demerara Mission, which was commenced nearly fifty years ago by the late excellent Rev. John Wray. The success which attended his labors and those of his honored successor, the Martyr-Missionary of Demerara, has seldom been exceeded in modern times. The result of their efforts was felt in the most remote districts of the colony. There are few aged people there who are not, directly or indirectly, indebted to the instrumentality of Wray, Smith, or Davies, for their knowledge of the truth and love of the Saviour. Many circumstances attending the revival of the East Coast Mission, in 1835, attest what a hold the truth, preached by those Missionaries, had obtained upon the minds of the people who had received it; while the means used show that the hearts of all men are in the Lord's hands, and that "he turneth them as the rivers of water."

Alexander Simpson, Esq., of Plantation Montrose and Ogle, acquired notoriety by having treated with great cruelty the

Missionary Mr. Smith, when he went to apprehend him, and adding insult to the sufferings of his scattered flock. When the effigy of Mr. Smith was suspended on a gallows in George Town, Mr. Simpson employed that barbarous deed to aggravate the bitter sufferings of the Christians attached to his property, by collecting them and reproachfully saying that *their parson was dead now, and they would get no more Missionary parsons in Demerara.* Some of the bereaved flock courageously replied, "Man kill the body, but can't hurt the soul."

Like Saul of Tarsus, who became the preacher of the faith he once labored to destroy, Mr. Simpson, in the wonderful course of providence, became himself a promoter of the cause of God, and the warm friend of the Missionary at Montrose. When attempts were made by Mr. Watt, in 1835, to revive the East Coast Mission, Mr. Simpson was the only proprietor who would consent to sell or grant a piece of land on which to erect a chapel. He gave freely four acres of land, at Plantation Montrose, to the London Missionary Society, for the erection of Mission premises. The attorneys of Plantation Le Resouvenir surrendered to Mr. Watt the old chapel built by Mr. Wray, and afterwards occupied by Mr. Smith. Mr. Wray had it removed to the front of Montrose. Never did any people undertake a work more cheerfully than did the surviving members of Mr. Smith's flock, with their families, accomplish the removal of their first sanctuary to the new site on Montrose. Not more joyfully did Israel remove the ark to Shiloh, than did these people carry, load after load, upon their heads, the timbers and boards of their Bethel, endeared to them by many melancholy associations, to its new resting-place. None but they who witnessed the deeply interesting scene on the day of its dedication can rightly conceive the emotions with which the once scattered flock assembled in their half finished sanctuary, and sang the memorable words of ancient Israel—

"Her dust and ashes that remain
Are precious to our eyes;

Those ruins shall be built again,
And all that dust shall rise."

Everywhere the joyful tidings spread, *"A' we Missionary parson come."* Week after week did the congregation increase; until, through the indefatigable efforts of Mr. Watt, the chapel, by repeated enlargements, occupied an area of 80 feet by 50. This capacious house was crowded on Lord's-days, large numbers being unable to find accommodation.

In a few years the Church and congregation at Montrose became very numerous. Many had to travel great distances to reach the chapel; Mr. Watt proposed, in consequence, a new station, farther up the coast, on Plantation Lusignan, land having been offered to the Society. Here the Writer, who had previously labored at Laguan and at Montrose, fixed his residence; when, on the 9th April, 1841, Zion Chapel, a commodious building, was opened for stated religious services.

The population of Buxton Village, about two miles from Lusignan, was increasing rapidly; and Zion Chapel being much too small for the congregation, the brethren strongly recommended the erection of another chapel, on land generously offered by the proprietors. On 24th November, 1843, the first stone was laid of a new chapel in Buxton, in the presence of a large assembly; on the 30th August following it was opened for divine worship, under the designation of *Arundel Chapel*—that mark of esteem being rendered to the Society's late honored Home Secretary.

The Church newly formed at Buxton comprised the majority of the members previously in connection with Zion Chapel. In the year 1840, with a view to concentrate the labors and promote the efficiency of the pastor and teachers, the members at Zion Chapel had been, by unanimous consent, incorporated with those at the new station.

Arundel Chapel stands in the midst of the free village of Buxton, on the east coast of Demerara. It is 70 feet by 40, with a deep end gallery. It can accommodate 700 persons, and is constantly well attended. The Sabbath School consists of nearly 500 children and others. There is a large Day School at Lusignan, and an Infant School at Buxton.

Since the erection of Arundel Chapel, the free village of Friendship has sprung up, contiguous to Buxton; both contain a population of 4,519. The line of the Demerara Railway passes through these villages. The locality promises soon to become one of the most populous districts of Guiana, George Town alone excepted. Buxton and Lusignan formed the sphere of Mrs. Henderson's labors.

A large and substantial chapel was commenced at Montrose by Mr. Watt, in 1843, previous to his leaving the colony through failure of health; it was finished in 1845. For several years, the villages of Beturnwagting on the east side of Montrose, and Plaisance on the west side, had been rapidly increasing in population; and for the convenience of the people residing in Beturnwagting, the chapel, being of wood, was literally moved from Montrose in 1851, by Mr. Hughes, the resident Missionary. A neat and commodious chapel was built in Plaisance Village, and opened on the 31st December, 1852. These villages on the east coast, with the estates in their neighborhood, contain a population of 16,647.

The present number of stations belonging to the London Missionary Society in Demerara is nine, and in Berbice ten. At these stations there are twenty-five Day Schools, attended by nearly 2,800 children. In the Sunday Schools there are 4,885 children and others, taught by nearly 300 teachers. At the end of last year there were 3,053 individuals in Christian fellowship.

Of the efficiency of the Day Schools belonging to the London Missionary Society, a gratifying testimony is given by George Dennis, Esq., the Government Inspector of Schools.[1]

1 The teachers who have had any sort of educational training are chiefly in connection with the Wesleyan and London Missionary bodies. . . . The teachers in connection with the London Missionaries have not in general, I believe, studied at any Normal Institution; but many have had

The schools belonging to the London Missionary Society have received very seasonable and valuable aid from the Society of Friends, for several years. But for this timely assistance many of these schools would have been greatly crippled, and in some instances they must have been discontinued. The fact that *all* other schools receive Government aid, with one exception (the school at Lusignan), will show how difficult it must be for voluntary schools to compete with such in a country like Guiana, where there are very few who render any assistance in the work of education.

---

the advantage of a careful training under these gentlemen, who, with an earnest desire for the extension and improvement of education, spare no labor in the frequent personal supervision and direction of their schools—which is the more valuable, as they have all more or less practically studied the art of teaching in the Normal Schools of England, with the express view to its application to this colony. . . . Among the schools best supplied with books are those of the London Missionaries, who procure from England the excellent series of the British and Foreign School Society, and have little difficulty in persuading the parents of the scholars to purchase them. . . . Galleries are almost confined to the schools of the Wesleyans and the London Missionaries. . . . Arithmetical bead-frames are rarely seen, except in the schools of the Wesleyans and London Missionaries. . . . Globes I have seen in two schools only (one of these belongs to the London Missionary Society). . . . Of one school in Berbice he says—"The children in the first class are reading in the Fourth Lesson Book, and Select English Poetry, and learning Cornwall's Grammar and Geography. They read remarkably well and distinctly, though, as usual, with a Creole accent. They write very fairly, and are as far advanced in arithmetic as reduction. In fact, the children in this school have made much more than the average progress. . . . I was much pleased with the neat appearance of the children in this school, and with the order and good discipline that prevailed."

Of another school he says—"The highest class is reading in the Fourth Lesson Book; is working sums in compound interest, discount, and mensuration; writes very well; and, besides the rudiments of grammar and geography, is learning music on Curwen's system."

CHAPTER 5

Candidate for Christian fellowship—Bible Lesson—First Communion Sabbath—Fruits of Labor—Failure of Health—Parting—Embarks for England—Domestic Sickness—Letters.

S ome of the most interesting traits of female character can only be observed while in their everyday employment. The "little drawer" in the senator's house gives an intensity of beauty and interest to that scene in the romantic escape of Eliza Harris.[1] The succeeding extracts from Mrs. Henderson's journal, written in snatches of time redeemed from rest, furnish some insight into the several departments of Missionary employment, at a time when the Montrose station demanded a large portion of her husband's attention; and they convey illustrations also of the kind of labor which she continued to perform till the week before her decease. The efforts she persisted in to benefit the children of Ham were not those of spasmodic excitement. They who witnessed the routine of her everyday employments could testify to the same amount of zeal which had characterized her earliest labors in the Demerara Mission. From a child she was energetic and persevering; and when she had consecrated her life unto the service of Christ, few things were undertaken without a perseverance which seldom relaxed.

---

1 In Mrs. Stowe's "Uncle Tom."

"*Saturday, the 6th.*—Had some interesting conversation with a poor woman today, one of the fruits of Mr. H.'s labors. She expressed her determination to forsake all for Christ. She said, 'it did not trouble her if she had not a plantain (the staple article of food) in the house: if she had Christ, she had everything.' Her deep penitence was expressed for her former sinful life, and I do hope she is really a brand plucked from the burning.

"*Sabbath, 7th.*—Summoned courage this morning, though with much trembling, to give the children a Scripture lesson in the gallery, in the end of the chapel. I might almost as well have gone into the pulpit, for nearly all the congregation were present, behind me. The day has been altogether one of peculiar excitement. After a deprivation of privileges of Christian communion at the Lord's table for two months, I sat down with this little band to celebrate the Lord's death. My feelings I will not attempt to describe—not a white countenance, but that of my dear husband's, present; but I felt that we were all one in Christ Jesus, and was enabled solemnly to renew my consecration to the service of Christ. *Union Street*, with all connected, was especially in my thoughts. God has indeed smiled upon this infant cause: eighty-five members have been added to the Church during the past year, while many are still inquiring the way to Zion.

"*Monday, 8th.*—Took a class of monitors, which I intend doing every day, if possible. In the evening attended our Missionary prayer meeting, which should have been held last Monday. The people here make a point of presenting their offerings to God on these occasions, after the manner of Old Testament times—'Bring an offering and come into my courts'; indeed, in this way all their contributions are made."

"*Sabbath, 28th.*—Gallery lesson in the morning. After service I took my adult class of Church members; and at five, the teachers, etc. Although I have talked incessantly in each of these lessons, I do not feel more tired than I was wont to do on Sabbath evening at home. Felt quite at home with the teachers, and hope I was enabled to make myself understood by them."

"*Tuesday, 30th.*—Gave the children of the Day School a gallery lesson. Was pleased with the attention and apparent interest with which they listened.

"*Wednesday, 31st.*—In the evening I took the first and second classes of the female Church members, prior to the celebration of the Lord's Supper. The whole Church meets thus every month, that they may receive special instruction in the doctrines and ordinances of the gospel."

These efforts, put forth by Mrs. Henderson, in the work of instruction, were followed by gratifying results. The Day and Sabbath Schools soon presented a marked and decided improvement as the fruits of her labors: the number of children increased, and the system of teaching became much more efficient.

The new Church which had been formed in Buxton Village added greatly to the labors of the Missionary and his wife: upon Mrs. H. had now devolved the superintendence of the Sabbath School at Lusignan. The Church and Sabbath School at Buxton had also a share of her attention. She frequently spent the Sabbath afternoon there, after her engagements at Lusignan. Such an amount of labor soon proved more than her strength could sustain.

Having suffered from repeated attacks of a threatening tendency, she was ordered, in the end of July, 1845, by medical advice, to proceed to England without delay. Stunned, at first, by advice given so imperatively, she soon admitted the necessity, which was visible to all her friends. With sorrowful reluctance she relinquished her interesting duties and cares, hoping it would be but for a season. When the people at the station were apprized of her resolution, consternation was added to their grief; since they learned that her husband was compelled to accompany her, and that he might not return; in which case they would be left without a pastor. The scene at Arundel Chapel on Sabbath, the 10th of August, would be difficult to describe. Whose eyes were not suffused with tears when parents and children crowded around the pastor's wife to say, or mean, "farewell"? The place was indeed a Bochim. Many of the affectionate and grateful old people, who had been but little accustomed to kindness in former days, wept bitterly at the thought that they would "never see Missee again;" while the young gave vent to their feelings in audible grief, on losing so soon a teacher who was endeared to them. Many hastened early to the Mission House the following day, to get a last look and hear the last word; several resolved, besides, to accompany their pastor and his family to the ship.

Mrs. Henderson and her husband, with their two children, embarked on board the *Claudia* on the 12th of August, 1845, and after a tedious passage arrived in London on the 30th of September.

After a sojourn of but two months, the Writer began his return to his sphere of labor, leaving his young children dangerously ill, and his beloved wife still in a critical state. The hour of parting must always, in similar circumstances, be painful; but no one can form an adequate idea of the pangs of that morning, when the afflicted wife bade her partner "farewell"; none truly, but such a wife, placed in such circumstances. And yet she never once said, "Stay till next packet." No; on the contrary, she said, "Go!" She was too considerate ever to allow her comfort or her wishes to interfere with her husband's work. This was, notwithstanding, the most trying part of her life; but yet the time when she experienced the value of a present God and Saviour. They who enjoy the happiness which conjugal life affords, the Writer feels persuaded, will require no apology, if he introduce a few extracts from letters written under these peculiarly trying circumstances. Such a companion helps to render this world both complacent and happy, while passing to the "better country." Mrs. Henderson was never more contented than when she denied herself, that she might contribute to the greater comfort and happiness of those she loved. Before she learned the doctrine of self-denial at the foot of the cross, she acted as an unselfish and affectionate child. She was ever watchful in anticipating the wishes of those endeared to her; and in a thousand ways did her genuine character and devotedness appear in those little things, which, when sweetened by genuine piety and sanctified by the divine blessing, constitute the balm of life.

"When I heard the door shut upon you, for a moment my heart sunk within me, though it was but for a moment; and then I made a great effort, I trust not in my own strength, to look forward to the time of our reunion; and I joyfully seized everything that was at all calculated to mitigate the trial of separation. Though I cannot say that the victory, that day, was all on one side, yet on the whole I had much cause for gratitude that He who had appointed the trial had mercifully sustained under it, and verified his own promise—'As thy day, so shall thy strength be.' The first thing that encouraged me was our dear Charlotte saying, shortly after you left, 'Mamma, I feel much better today.' After the very gloomy apprehensions that had filled my mind the day before, as I saw her tossing to and fro in all the restlessness of fever, and then thought of what might be the possible result to her weak frame, you can believe how cheering these few words were. When Mr. Hooper came he seemed much surprised, and kindly inquired if you had seen the favorable change; and said, sympathizingly, 'Poor fellow! I pitied him much, last night.'

"When the postman knocked, on Wednesday, I hardly dared hope; but, oh, the joy, to see a letter from your own dear self! This strengthened my resolution; was renewed cause for gratitude to the God of our lives; and led me to hope that what had begun so well would terminate equally so. If ever I felt the value of the post, it was at that moment.

"What shall I say about the unexpected treat of Thursday—your letter by the pilot? It was kind; and how valued, I cannot tell. Charlotte asked what sort of a voyage you had had. She did not seem, the first day, to understand at all that you had really left; and in her feverish dreams at night, she ever and anon asked if papa was coming soon. Poor child! she understands it now.

"How much, my own love, did I wish to have been with you yesterday (Sabbath), to have united with you at the throne of grace, as we have done in days gone by! I could almost fancy, at times, I felt your arm encircling, and heard your voice; but it was a delusion. But of this I was quite sure, that we were not forgotten by you, any more than you were by us. How great is the privilege of spreading the condition of those whom we love before our Father's throne! I have been wondering where you are at this time; perhaps on deck, in some warm latitude, thinking of the coming Sabbath, and wishing you could spend it at Lusignan: that wish will, I hope, soon be granted, and then I pray that you may have abundant reason to rejoice in the evidence of the Lord being with you in deed and of a truth. May your message of the 'true and faithful saying' lead many to the Saviour. Dwell much upon the fact that 'Christ Jesus came into the world to save sinners.' God is glorified when his Son is exalted, and by lifting up the Saviour sinners are attracted. I long to hear that the Churches are being increased with pious people, whose influence shall be exerted on the side of truth. I hope some of the young people will give you encouragement."

The next time that Mrs. Henderson made use of her pen was to record the goodness of God after passing through severe personal affliction, and after the protracted illness of her two children.

"O my dear love, how did I miss you! I wanted your dear hand to grasp, and your own dear shoulder to lean my aching head upon. Perhaps it was well I had not these, or I might not have been enabled so entirely to have stayed my mind upon God. I do indeed feel thankful to be able to record that I found the truth of the Psalmist's words—'God is our refuge and *strength*, a very *present help* in trouble.' He was indeed present when those whom I most loved were far away.

"Let me entreat of you, my beloved husband, to pray earnestly and constantly that this renewed stroke may be sanctified to us all. I desire, for myself, to feel deeply humbled that my sins should render such repeated tokens necessary. O that I had profited by former afflictions! then perhaps had the present been spared. In looking back upon the past, I see so much that has been imperfect and positively sinful, in the discharge of the various relations of life, as a wife, a mother, and a teacher, etc., that I wonder not that God should smite—my wonder would be, did I not know his character, that he 'in wrath should remember mercy.' That he has done it, is a subject of adoring gratitude; and I earnestly pray that my future life may evidence the deep sense of thankfulness which I trust my heart feels. I am now more anxious than ever to rejoin you, and try and be of some service to you in our Master's work. Oh, I do hope you will be made very useful, very successful, as a preacher of the gospel, as a teacher of the young and ignorant, etc. May the blessing of the Most High be richly poured out upon you!

"I am truly thankful now, my dearest love, that you left by the first December mail, as you were thus saved much anxiety which you must otherwise have felt, had you left me, as you would have been obliged to have done, on the 17th; and no doubt it would have been much worse for me. God orders all things well. I feel that I can more than ever trust him. I cannot tell you how often I think of Sir Walter Scott's remark, after the death of Lady Scott—'that he had no inducement to be ill, as there was no one to come and arrange his pillow for him.' Unless I asked, no one ever thought of changing my pillows for days together; not from any want of kindness, but from not being accustomed to *fiddle faddle* with fidgetty invalids. You know I am not very particular about my pillows. Do not think, my dearest, that I write complainingly; quite the contrary—it is more for amusement than anything, and is, I fear, a very useless consumption of your time to peruse. After all the abundant mercies of my heavenly Father, it would be indeed base ingratitude in me to complain of anything. So long as God deals not with me according to my sins, nor towards me according to my iniquities, I desire to feel that everything is of mercy. Then let me call upon you to 'magnify the Lord with me: let us exalt his name together.' Together in *person*, we cannot, but in heart we may; and I do hope, before another year, we may kneel at that dear spot where we have so often together bowed the knee and poured out our united breathings. Do not let the old couch be removed; it is dear to me from a thousand associations. It was by its side that we first together knelt (I refer not, of course, to family worship), in our new relation to each other. O for such another occasion! I shall love to think of you as kneeling there."

"*March* 31, 1846 . . . I cannot but hope that our dear C—— is very susceptible to the reception of the truth. I trust her conscience is tender, and that she cherishes the desire to be a child of God. She said the other evening, when I was putting her to bed, 'Mamma, the best thing you can hear of me, when we are separated, is, that I am a child of God, and that I am attending to my lessons.' God grant that this may be our unspeakable happiness in reference to both our dear children; and then we may safely leave them in the hands of our heavenly Father, who will do for them better than we can. We must be more earnest in prayer for them; and show that we desire their salvation, by affectionately urging religious truths upon their minds. I sometimes think that, had I been less of a *teacher*, I should have been a better *mother*. I do not wonder that so many teachers live and die in '*single* blessedness,' as the phrase goes. I prefer the *double* state, and bless God for the day which made me your wife, and you my own precious but too indulgent husband. Should I be spared to return, it shall be my study to return all your love, and to assist you in your delightful work. O how I long for this! I feel that it will make amends for all, to lay my head upon your loving breast. . . . I commend you and all our interests, yonder and here, to the God of love. May he bless, preserve, sanctify, sustain, and keep you! Be watchful, be careful, be faithful. 'Faithful is he who has called' you to his service. On his promises we rely; they are like himself, faithful and true. Only let us be found faithful, and our God will not forsake us."

During the summer months of 1846, Mrs. Henderson spent some days at Belper and Hartlepool with very dear friends, from whom she received great kindnesses. At the latter place she was warmly welcomed and entertained by an early friend, to whom she was tenderly attached. After spending a few weeks pleasantly and profitably in the north of England, she proceeded to Aberdeen, where her younger child had been left the year before. A deputation from the London Missionary Society visited that city while she was there, which was deeply interesting to her.

Although suffering from physical weakness, Mrs. Henderson frequently employed her pen during her residence in Britain; addressed counsels to mothers and other female members of the Church left behind her at Buxton; and composed hymns and catechisms, in simple language, for their schools. Indeed, such was her anxiety to benefit the Church and schools at the stations, that she never allowed a packet to leave Southampton for Demerara without a contribution from her pen, touching on the subject of instruction; while she was also ever on the look out for a new book, or what else might assist to advance education.

Her husband strongly advised her not to leave England before September or October; but such was her anxiety at being from home, that, on hearing of a vessel about to leave in August for Demerara, she decided to return. Short as the time was, she had to place her elder daughter at Walthamstow, besides preparing for the voyage.

CHAPTER 6

Arrives at Lusignan—Resumes her Work—Forms new Plans of Usefulness—Senior Bible Class—New Class Room—Death of an Elder Girl—Candidates for Fellowship—Visit to a Dying African— Scenes on a Sugar Plantation—Coolie Immigration.

While engaged with a class in the Day School, on the morning of the 29th of September, 1846, the Writer was astonished at hearing some boys exclaiming, *"Missee is come!"* It was so; for on looking towards the Mission House he beheld his beloved wife and their dear child at the door. Such was the first intimation he had of their arrival in Guiana.

The Sabbath following, Mrs. Henderson resumed her duties in the Sabbath School, all of whom rejoiced to see their teacher again. Never did a teacher show greater real pleasure than she did; hers was "a labor of love."

The Day School also received a large portion of her attention— the fruits of which were soon manifest, in improved appearance, and in increase of attendants. Among the mothers in the Church and the young females in the Bible class, new plans of usefulness were introduced, to make them better mothers, and such as "women professing godliness" ought to be.

The want of suitable domestic training and discipline had hith-erto been a serious hindrance to the progress of instruction. To aid mothers in training their children for God, by suggestions, counsels, reading, etc., she formed a Maternal Association, which met regularly every week. To have expected the same kind of results from this weekly gathering as similar efforts have produced in England, is more than the peculiarities of West Indian life would justify. Still good was accomplished, and their teacher was greatly encouraged.

A select class was also formed by Mrs. Henderson, for the special benefit of young women who had few or no advantages, owing to the nature of their employment in agriculture or other branches of labor. The instruction given in this class, and the interest it excited in these young women, helped very much to create a taste for reading in the Sabbath Schools. Here the teacher came into closer contact with her pupils, and failed not to exercise her influence for their good. This class afforded opportunities of recommending books and maps, with other helps in acquiring knowledge, which could not have been employed on the Sabbath. The steady and regular attendance of those young women, many of whom had walked three or four miles after laboring under a tropical sun all day, proved the interest they felt. Mrs. Henderson sometimes used Dr. Brewer's valuable "Questions" in her class; and her class might have been heard discussing, on their way home, some philosophic doctrine, such as "the cause of hunger," "the properties of the atmosphere," etc.

With a view to provide more efficiently for the Church and congregation assembling in Zion Chapel, Lusignan, it had been decided, as already stated, at the close of 1846, to incorporate that Church with the one at Arundel Chapel, Buxton. Thus the labors of pastor and teachers were concentrated. Most of the congregation met regularly three times every Lord's-day, for instruction and worship.

A wider and more important sphere was opened also for the pastor's wife, which she cheerfully and efficiently occupied. The more intelligent young people she formed into a large Bible class; and notwithstanding the many opposing circumstances which militated against her usefulness, the Writer has never seen the young of his congregation take a greater interest in any of the stated religious services.

The exhaustion incident to teaching a class of 60 or 70 in the chapel, where nearly 500 persons, young and old, were receiving simultaneous and, in some classes, collective instruction, suggested the desirableness of providing a separate building for Mrs. Henderson's Bible class. No sooner was this proposed to the members of that class, than a subscription commenced for its erection, which they prosecuted with earnestness. Nearly the entire cost was contributed by themselves. A commodious room was accordingly soon built, which continues to afford great facilities in teaching. Many sought admission into the select Bible class, and the time and labor expended upon it were not lost. The great interest excited in that class was sustained up to the week of their teacher's death. The secret of this was the thorough preparedness of every lesson taught in it, and the other means employed by the teacher for benefiting those under her care.

Mrs. Henderson's anxiety for the salvation of those around her will be seen by an entry in her journal on the sudden death of a young woman belonging to her class, which occurred during the time of the morning school exercises:—

"*Sabbath*, *28 April*.—This has been to me a solemn day. One of the most tiresome and thoughtless of my class has been suddenly called into the eternal world. I cannot hope she was prepared. I am overwhelmed with the thought that she was in my class—that I shall never again be permitted to point her to the Saviour. O that I had been more affectionately faithful, more instant in season and out of season! I felt almost afraid to teach this afternoon. I was indeed thankful that allusion to Sophia R——'s death seemed to produce an impression upon the class, most of whom were in tears. May the painful event bring life to some! They feel much for the poor mother, who was in a great measure dependent upon her daughter's industry."

"*Monday, 29th.*—S. R——'s funeral at Buxton. As there were many young people present, Mr. H. and Mr. S—— sought to turn the painful event into an occasion for good. It has certainly produced a strong sensation among the young."

Two weeks after this entry, she wrote:—"N. N—— and A. M—— applied for admission into the candidates' class. These are interesting youths, especially the latter, from my Bible class. They profess to have come to a decision in consequence of the sudden death of S. R——. I have for some time past regarded these youths with hope. When such as these express a determination to proceed Zionward, we cannot help feeling much trembling anxiety for them. So many, who began well, have turned aside, and no longer walk with God's people, that we are ofttimes afraid to hold out that encouragement which is so warmly given in other lands. None but residents in this country can form an idea of its dire temptations to the young, just emerging from youth into active life. May the Keeper of Israel preserve them as his own!"

Mrs. Henderson was seldom mistaken in the opinion she formed of individual character. The latter of these two youths has for several years adorned his Christian profession by a consistent walk under circumstances peculiarly trying. He has also been one of the most exemplary teachers in Buxton Sabbath School. Indeed, the best of the teachers in that school had been members of Mrs. H.'s select Bible class.

Among all who attended the chapel at Buxton, there were not any with whom Mrs. Henderson sympathized more than with the good aged and tried people of a former generation, who had endured bitter persecution. In the following extract she gave utterance to these feelings toward an excellent woman of simple piety:—

"At the close of the afternoon school, I accompanied my husband to visit N. S——, a good old woman, who appears at the threshold of heaven. She is very happy, and longing to depart and to be with Christ. During her life she has had much trouble, from her husband and several ungodly children. It is sad to witness the callousness and ingratitude of many grown-up children to their poor old parents. While in some things the young people are before the old, yet in most of the sterling qualities they are far behind. That determination to be independent of all control, the natural result of a transition from cruel thraldom, causes them to appear in a very unfavorable point of view. The piety of the old is perhaps not so intelligent as that of the young, but in many cases it produces far better fruits."

She appreciated the obstructions which impeded Missionary enterprise, arising from the social relations of the inhabitants. An incident occurred on a visit to George Town, which Mrs. Henderson describes in a significant manner:—

"Had a sharp run for the train. The streets being too wet for baby to walk, and Anne being very tired, Mr. H. at one time took them both up in his arms. A sight so novel as a *white man* carrying his two children amused the black people amazingly, and various were the odd, joking remarks which they made. Very few white men, in this wicked land, have been distinguished for their affectionate care of their children. In most cases, the hue of their skin, proclaiming their descent from an African mother, has made them ashamed of them. There are exceptions, but few indeed."

A detail of facts witnessed on a sugar plantation will exhibit what followed the introduction of heathens and some infidels among a half enlightened peasantry; and will also show the demoralizing and retrograding influences by which the native laborers on many estates are actually surrounded.

"Paid my first visit to —— this morning, to visit some sick

members of the Church. Grieved to see the uncomfortable houses in which some excellent old people are living. Many of the respectable negroes, faithful servants for many years on the estate, are worse housed than the filthy Coolies. O what sights of filth and misery do these *Coolie ranges* exhibit! Almost without exception, the inhabitants closely approached a state of nudity. I felt sorry that our children should witness these scenes. But the worst of all is, that these wretched, idolatrous, debased outcasts, have no one to prove to them that their souls are cared for."

The effects of Coolie immigration on the country have been most disastrous. The native population needed none to help them in their downward career. What the end of these things will be is sad to think of. It is to be feared the Churches have a trying season to pass through. Much dross will be lost, but the precious metal will remain. Our *work* will be tested as by fire—perhaps, too, *we* ourselves. Shall *it* abide? shall *we* be found faithful?[1]

To Miss F——, a much esteemed friend who rendered essential help to the schools at Lusignan and Buxton, Mrs. Henderson wrote, in October, 1847—

"You will be glad to know that the package so kindly forwarded by you came safe to hand on the 30th ult. Of its contents I know not how to write, so as to convey to you the sense we entertain of its value. To the British and Foreign School Society we desire to tender our grateful thanks for the valuable and seasonable supply of books,

[1] Apart from the injurious effects of excessive taxation, which the immigration scheme renders necessary, the introduction of hordes of ignorant, idolatrous, and sensual immigrants, is of itself operating most powerfully against the prosperity of the Mission Churches. A tide of ungodliness and immorality has set in, which threatens to sweep away the work of years; and the Missionaries laboring in British Guiana need at the present time most peculiarly the sympathy and prayers, and in many cases the pecuniary contributions, of the friends of Missions in the mother country.— *"The Demerara Martyr."* By Rev. E. N. Wallbridge. W. and F. G. Cash.

lessons, etc. The grant from the 'Friends' Fund' is invaluable. Such beautiful maps have never been seen by any of our scholars before. . . . The new lessons published by the Christian Knowledge Society are just what we wanted, to explain many things which are subjects of lessons, but of which the children here cannot form any conception. It was only last week that I was lamenting the impossibility of conveying to their minds any idea of the glaciers, or of an avalanche. Your own gift of Infant School lessons, etc. will be of very great use to us. We deeply feel your kindness, in giving so much time and taking so much trouble in procuring and forwarding these things. I trust we shall be able from time to time to give you accounts of the usefulness of our schools. We are very anxious about the young. There is so much in the domestic and social habits of the people calculated to counteract all our teaching, that, even when we see the bud of *promise*, we rejoice with trembling. Few in England can form any idea of the state of morals in the West Indies. Long, long, we fear, it will be, before slavery's accursed fruits will disappear from this land. Morality was at a low ebb enough before the monstrous immigration schemes came into force; but crime has fearfully increased since the large influx of Coolies and Portuguese. The children of the immigrants do not, generally, attend any schools, and the parents indulge in the most filthy habits.

"From the papers you will see how our people are being oppressed by various *ordinances* passed by the planter legislature of this country. The last of these, viz., the 'Tax Ordinance,' presses most heavily upon our poor people. You are aware that some years ago the tyranny of the planters drove many of the people to the purchasing of lots of land. These they have planted with provisions, and looked to the sale of the surplus provisions to help to support their families. By the new law, the people are prohibited from selling the smallest quantity of any kind of provisions, without a license of ten dollars. Petitions against this law are being forwarded to Earl Grey; but we do not look for much redress until our government is entirely changed, and a House of Assembly granted, with an extension of the franchise.

"The movement which I think I mentioned as having commenced among the young, is going on quietly. We pray that it may result in many confessing Christ, not with the lips only, but with the heart and life.

"We had a public examination of the school in August. It was conducted almost entirely by the teacher, and gave great satisfaction. The girls exhibited needlework which pleased their mothers much.

"The early age at which the children leave the school to go to work is a serious evil, and very discouraging to a teacher. The wages which children receive are much better, in proportion, than those of adults, which induce many parents with large families to send their children at an early age to the estates. Soon much of what they had learnt at school is forgotten; and, what is worse, their morals in many cases become seriously corrupted by associating with the depraved characters who are to be met with on every estate. But for the Sabbath Schools, we should to a great extent lose sight of those children who leave the Day Schools. Meeting with them on the Sabbath gives us the opportunity of warning and exhorting them, and is, I believe, no small restraint upon many.

"Two of the Coolie children respecting whom I wrote to you, are now in the school. The little boy is very sharp, and has in the course of three months learned to read in the Second Lesson Book. We have also a Portuguese girl. The instances of the children of immigrants attending school are so rare, that we feel an unusual interest in these children, and cannot help hoping that they may be as the little leaven that leaveneth the whole lump."

But for the timely and important aid which has been for several years rendered by those steadfast advocates of the African race, "the Society of Friends," to the Mission Schools in Guiana, many of them would have been seriously crippled, and some must have been closed. It is almost impossible, without those and other providential supplies, for voluntary schools to be conducted with efficiency in a country like Guiana, where a teacher has to contend with schools upheld by a system alike unjust and oppressive, and which places him under so great a disadvantage that nothing but love for his Saviour enables him to contend with it.

CHAPTER 7

A Mother's Fears—Leguan Island—Prayer Meetings—Disappointed Hopes—Punctuality and System—Preparation for her Class—Mode of Teaching—Anne's Illness—An Evil Dreaded—Birth of her Third Child—Review of the Past—Watch Service—New Year—A Mother's First Grief.

ANNE ELIZA, Mrs. Henderson's firstborn, was a child of many prayers. She caused her mother constant solicitude, in consequence of early indications of having somehow been dreadfully frightened: she frequently awoke at night in terror and unconsciousness. Her watchful mother dreaded imbecility, and was for many months filled with distress respecting her child, as her journal shows.

"*Tuesday,* 18th (*July,* 1850).—Dear Anne's birthday. Three years ago, how joyful was the feeling that she was born! From her birth she has enjoyed excellent health. This is a cause for much thankfulness. Why then am I so 'cast down'? Shall I write the dreadful fear that haunts my mind and destroys my peace? Yes, I will write, and try to look at it firmly; it is this—I fear that in our dear Anne there is a tendency to *imbecility.* I never thought so until her frights. For some time I hoped that the peculiar movement of her eyes was simply muscular, or habit formed in the frights referred to. My dear husband cannot see the least ground for fear. I am glad he cannot. He is happier for it; and it certainly would aggravate my fears, did he seem alarmed. This is my burden: why should I carry it, when my heavenly Father commands me to *roll it upon him?* I will try."

At the mouth of the Essequibo River is situate the lovely island of Leguan, the scene of the Writer's early labors in Guiana. This interesting spot was a sphere of Missionary labor in the days of Mr. Smith, the *"Demerara Martyr."* The Mission here was revived in 1835, by the Rev. R. B. Taylor, now of South Africa. During the Writer's residence, the sea dam broke, and the Mission premises thereby became uninhabitable. The people connected with the station were visited by the brethren in Demerara as often as practicable. In 1842, the Rev. S. S. Murkland, now in the United States, succeeded, after encountering great difficulties and enduring much personal labor and anxiety, in removing the Mission premises to a more populous part of the island. The small Church at Leguan has been without a resident pastor since Mr. Murkland's departure from the colony; but the Missionaries were accustomed to visit the station, as circumstances permitted.

Arrangements were made for holding a series of meetings at Urwick Chapel, Leguan, in the month of August, 1850. The weather being favorable, this opportunity of getting a little change, by water, was gladly embraced by the two Mission families on the east coast of Demerara. A brief account of their visit, taken from Mrs. Henderson's journal, is here inserted.

"Tuesday, 6th.—Left town at two p.m., in the sloop *Catherine,* Capt. Wellington. It had been raining all the morning, but cleared up before going on board. We had a tedious but in other respects pleasant passage, and landed at Endeavour a little after seven; we found several kind friends waiting for us on the shore. There being a meeting in the chapel, Mr. Hughes and Mr. Henderson went to it, while Mrs. Hughes and I should see our little ones to rest. I trust

we all feel disposed to erect our Ebenezer to the 'God of the sea and of the dry land.'

"*Wednesday, 7th.*—Enjoyed a walk with the children. In this respect Leguan is far superior to the coast of Demerara. The public road is agreeably shaded with wild olive trees. The people's provision grounds, too, are near the road, which give the locality an inhabited appearance. In the time of slavery, Leguan no doubt deserved its appellation of 'Garden of Guiana,' when the whole island was highly cultivated. Even now it is pretty, although so flat."

"*Sabbath, 11th.*—First sound this morning was the bell for the early prayer meeting. Prayer meetings are frequently denominated the pulse, the thermometer, of the Church. In some places this no doubt is true; but I do not think it holds good here, especially in reference to *morning prayer meetings*. These meetings had their origin in the dark days of slavery. They were then a good. Few among the people on an estate could lead devotional exercises: these few conducted the meetings for 'morning and evening praise.' The colored people, above all others, are creatures of habit; hence they still like morning meetings. In many cases these meetings are an excuse for the nonobservance of family worship, even by professing Christians; others make them an excuse for late attendance at the Sabbath School and public worship. The bulk of the people attend these meetings in *déshabillé*. They then go saunteringly home, bathe, dress, etc.; and when the bell rings for school, their toilet is perhaps scarcely begun. So it is here. I observed some Sabbath School teachers coming to their classes from *half an hour* to an *hour and a half* after the time the Sabbath School professes to commence; nor were many of the children or adults better than their teachers. I felt it strange to have nothing to do either morning or afternoon, being accustomed to my large class at home."

"*Saturday, 16th.*—All our arrangements were made for leaving the island today. Our passage taken; weather appeared unfavorable; still we hoped it would clear. About twelve noon, dear baby was laid down with fever; and at one, Anne began to complain of being poorly. She was laid on the sofa, and almost immediately a severe fit came on. Usual remedies were resorted to, but the convulsions lasted a long time, and severe agitation and unconsciousness much longer. 'The thing that I greatly feared is come upon me.' I feel persuaded there is a connection between the fit and the frights so often alluded to, and that the former is the development of the latter. Joan has just complained of fever. Thus in a few short hours are all our dear children laid down one after another, our plans of returning home thwarted, and we are taught how easily God can frustrate all our purposes. Still we see mercy in this dispensation. Had we been already in the ship, when our dear little ones were taken sick, how aggravated would have been the affliction! Our heavenly Father doeth all things well. O that this fainting heart could trust him more!"

That one who was noted for her punctuality in everything, and especially in her attendance at the house of God, should have noticed and deplored the late attendance of teachers, etc., is not to be wondered. Mrs. Henderson never allowed her class, on Sabbath or during the week, to wait for her. Whoever was late at chapel or school, she was sure to be in time. Her pastor was never grieved, nor the worship of God disturbed, by her late attendance at the sanctuary. So punctual was she in all her engagements and correspondence, that the Writer never knew her to be late for post, or train, or journeys by land or water, but once, and that was in consequence of her depending upon a friend to send a cab to take her to the train. It mattered not with whom she made an appointment, whether a lady or a poor Sunday School girl, she was alike punctual, and never gave any person occasion to wait her.

Of all countries, there is no place where punctuality is more needed in ministers and teachers than the West Indies, where there is frequently so much sauntering, and where time is so little valued. It is no uncommon thing for a minister to receive a message at half past seven, a.m., to attend a funeral, perhaps several miles'

distance, at eight o'clock; and after hastening to the place of interment, he may have to wait in the hot sun or rain until ten or eleven
o'clock. A boy makes his appearance at the door of the Mission
House, demands a sight of the "parson," and forthwith delivers a
message he received from his "uncle," to the effect that the minister
is wanted at chapel at eleven o'clock, to perform an important and
interesting service. True to his promise, he reaches the chapel at the
hour named, but the wedding party may not make their appearance
much before one!

Many people, who witnessed Mrs. Henderson's regular and
punctual attendance at school and chapel every Sabbath, wondered
how she could devote so much of that day to teaching (generally
eight or nine consecutive hours, including the time of public worship), at a distance of nearly two miles from the Mission House. But
the secret of all this, and a great deal more which she accomplished,
was her *system*. It was no more difficulty for her, with four young
children (and one a babe, a few weeks old), to be present every
Sabbath morning at eight o'clock at the teachers' prayer meeting,
than it would be for some mothers to get to chapel five minutes
past eleven. From the time her children were a few weeks old, they
regularly accompanied their dear mother to the Sabbath School and
to chapel. She never lost a sermon, nor her class a lesson, because
she had a babe to nurse and a young family to attend to.

Her system was carried into everything that she undertook. She
had a time for everything, and generally everything was done in its
own time. One part of each day was given to secret devotion and
family prayer; another to domestic duties and work; another part to
the instruction of her children, and the girls in the Day School; a
certain portion was allotted for reading (she was a great reader); and
when not engaged with meetings or evening classes, she devoted a
part of each evening to the instruction of her children and household. After her children retired, she was either employed in preparing for her classes, or reading or writing, when alone; which was
frequent, from her husband's numerous and late engagements at

Buxton and elsewhere. Mrs. Henderson had also fixed days and eve-nings for certain kinds of work, and seldom was one duty allowed to clash with another.

The work of the Sabbath School was sure not to be deferred, and was never undertaken without due preparation. Saturday night never found her unprepared for the work of the following day. She was ever gleaning from all sources for her classes. Whatever facts in history, biography, science, or the customs and manners of nations, helped to confirm or elucidate the doctrines of revelation, were called to her aid. The best of English periodicals were read; and whatever she met with in them calculated to illustrate the truth taught, was made good use of. She was one who thought for herself, but thankfully availed herself of all the helps which came in her way. This was followed by thorough and searching questioning, and close application of the truth to the hearts and consciences of all in her class. The tender and faithful appeals made by the affection-ate teacher were such as even the deceitful heart could not elude, and seldom failed, it is believed, to produce convictions "of sin, of righteousness, and of judgment." It was scarcely possible for a guilty conscience to sit under her teaching with peace, while the awakened or inquiring soul was sure to hear something suited to her case.

Mrs. Henderson constantly aimed at the conversion of every soul in her class; and the truth was presented in a clear, simple, and interesting way, calculated to win the heart and impress the conscience. In her teaching was combined tenderness with impres-sive earnestness; she possessed much discernment of character, and power of adapting her instructions to all characters, classes, and ages. The doctrine of the Cross was frequently introduced, and dwelt upon with tenderness and faithfulness; and her class was seldom allowed to separate without being solemnly reminded of death, eternity, and judgment. So great was her anxiety to make her instructions sufficiently plain and simple that everyone in her class might understand them, that she frequently wrote carefully prepared questions, adapted to the several capacities of her charges.

Probably most intelligent teachers in England would consider this superfluous; but to many of the Creoles of Guiana the plainest questions are frequently not understood, except when put in a particular form.

The Writer has listened (unknown) to Mrs. Henderson while engaged in her class, and can say without exaggeration that he never heard the doctrines of the gospel taught with more interesting and impressive clearness and simplicity, communicated in language which all might understand, and accompanied with tender and faithful appeals to the hearts and consciences of her charge. None were passed over; everyone, whatever her character or station, received a portion. The fact is, Mrs. Henderson never gave her class that which cost her nothing. She generally brought out of the vast treasure "things new and old." The Writer has often coveted her talent in adapting her instructions so well to the capacities, ages, and characters of her class.

Under the following dates, Mrs. Henderson wrote thus:—

"*Sabbath* (*25th August*, 1850).—All ready to set out for Buxton, when baby was taken with ague: I and the two little ones therefore remained at home. They were both *very ill* until the afternoon. I fear there is much rebellion in my heart. I cannot feel at all satisfied that my darling little ones should return to God who gave them. The possibility of such a termination to their sickness causes my 'spirit within me to be overwhelmed, my heart within me to be desolate.' But why should I expect to be exempt from the severe trials which have fallen upon others? I deserve the rod, for I have strayed too long. O that affliction may do its work, in leading back my wandering heart to the Shepherd and Bishop of souls!"

. . . "This has been a day of intense anxiety. Yesterday, soon after the commencement of the Sabbath School, both the little ones were laid down with fever. This proved very obstinate, especially in dear Anne. It broke in the afternoon, but both went to bed with hot fever. Anne's lasted all night, and up to breakfast time this morning, when she had a severe fit. The convulsions were not so strong as the last, but I felt more alarmed even than then, from the overwhelming feeling that I had, that the fit had left her an *idiot*. Oh, how bitter was the feeling! I will not attempt to describe. I tried to realize the lesson I attempted to teach yesterday, from *Aaron's holding his peace* when Nadab and Abihu were slain; and the parallelism—'I opened not my mouth, because thou didst it.' At half past two, p.m., she showed signs of consciousness, by asking for her 'thimble' and 'bag.' 'Bless the Lord, O my soul, and forget not all his benefits.' . . .

"On Thursday, November 14th, at 11¾, p.m., God graciously built up our household by giving us another precious babe, a darling daughter. We receive her as our heavenly Father's gift, and desire only permission to train her for himself. But, oh, the responsibility of this charge! He who gave us our little ones alone can give us grace to teach them the good and the right way. . . .

"It has been amusing to listen to the droll remarks of our visitors, on the sex of our dear babe. 'Girl! girl! nothing but girl! Can't get a parson for a' we,' etc. The black people speak very disparagingly of girls. 'Man' is here truly 'lord of the creation.' Sisters wait on their brothers, and wives on their husbands, as if the former were intended to be slaves of the latter. Of course there are exceptions to this, as to every rule."

"*Sabbath.*—Our darling babe was this day presented to God in baptism. God gave her to us, and we have, I trust, in faith given her back to God, and humbly pray to be allowed to train her, with our other dear ones, for his service. How heavy is my responsibility! My spirit sinks within me. 'O Lord, undertake for me!'"

"*Friday, 13th December.*—Seven years today I landed on this shore. In reviewing these years, there is much, very much, for devout gratitude to the God of all grace and comfort. Our house has been built up, which at one time seemed very improbable. Our health has been generally good, and 'no good thing' has our God 'withheld from us.' But there is also much cause for sadness and humiliation. When I left England, I hoped and expected to do much; now I feel that I have done nothing, and my sphere of public usefulness seems contracting. Seven years ago, the Church was large and seemed lively. It has decreased every year to the present. I sometimes fear I am the 'Achan' in the camp of Israel—that I have hindered when I should have helped. Again and again do I devise plans for increasing my efficiency in various departments of duty. How often have my evenings been planned out for devotional and other exercises; and when all the children are in bed, I feel so thoroughly exhausted that nothing is done! I write this by guess, for my head and eyes are aching, and I feel so thoroughly weary that I can scarcely guide my pen."

"*Tuesday*, 24*th*.—My dear husband is in town, attending one of a series of meetings to be held in Smith Chapel, this week. It is very certain that revivals are needed, greatly needed, in all the Churches of this land. The kingdom of Christ does not appear to be advancing. It becomes us to inquire, 'Wherefore dost thou contend with us?' Is there not in us much that may cause the refreshing showers to be withheld? 'Come, thou north wind; and blow, thou south.' I feel painfully that the work of God needs to be revived in my own heart. Shall it not be revived? What is there to hinder?

"*Wednesday*, 25*th* (commonly called '*Christmas-day*').—How altered are our circumstances from what they were this day five years—my husband upon the sea, myself very ill in bed, our two children both in a precarious state after severe fever! Then there was little prospect of our house being built up. Since that time, three dear little ones have been added to our number; and though our cares and anxieties are thereby increased, our joys are so too. I sometimes fear lest God should be dealing with me in judgment rather than mercy. He gave the Israelites their request, but sent leanness into their soul. My heart appears so unmoved by all these mercies!

"*Tuesday*, 31.—

'And now, my soul, another year
Of thy short life is past.

I cannot long continue here,
And this may be my last.'

Yes; in less than three short hours this year will be numbered with the things that have been. What is to be recorded of the year 1850? It has been a year of much, very much, mercy. It is true, our cup has been mingled, and, to myself, a portion of this year has been the most anxious of my life. But though our dear children were afflicted, there has not only been no breach, but our family has been built up. Could I think of my heavenly Father's mercies, my heart would be filled with joy; but when I realize my shortcomings, I feel sad, and covered with shame. Oh, why have I been borne with? Others have been cut off—why not I? My *personal* sins have been numerous and aggravated; my shortcomings as a *wife*, a *mother*, a *teacher of others*, have been very great. Yet God has spared to me my beloved husband, my dear children, and has not laid me low by affliction. What shall I render unto the Lord for all his benefits? Shall the coming year be spent as the past? God forbid. O for grace to form and keep holy resolutions for the future!

"My dear husband is now on his way to Buxton, to hold a special meeting after the manner of the 'Wesleyans' watch night.' He is very anxious for the result of this, which to the bulk of our people is entirely new. Our hope is, that the *novelty* may arrest some, who seem to have become hardened under ordinary means. I wish I could meet with them; but though this is denied me, I may meet with God, and thus have fellowship with them.

'Prayer shall a vast triangle form,
On whose broad base we all may meet.'

I would thus try to catch a few drops of the copious shower which I cannot but hope will fall, in answer to special, earnest, united, importunate prayer.

"*Wednesday, January 1st.*—The meeting held last night and

this morning, to lead to consideration respecting the past and the future, was very numerously attended. Mr. Simon (the catechist) addressed sinners and unfruitful professors very faithfully, from 'the barren fig tree;' and Mr. H. spoke from the words—'The harvest is past, and the summer is ended, and we are not saved.' O that good may result!

"Today three backsliders came: viz., L. D——, T. S——, and J. ——. Regarding the first of these, we indulge the hope that his repentance is sincere; there is a subduedness of manner about him which he never before exhibited. I have more hope of him now than I had when he was first received into the Church. The others give but little evidence of true repentance—the last especially, who inquired if he 'had not now been *time enough* out of the Church?' I fear too many look upon Church discipline as a sort of penance, to be endured for a certain time; and when a moderate time has passed, all is right. Hence many, when they find that readmission into the Church cannot be obtained on these terms, go over to those places where access to religious ordinances is very easy, character not being of much account, and genuine godliness of no account at all.

"*Thursday, 2nd.*—Conversed with L——, one of the young people in the candidates' class. Her knowledge is not great, but she appears to feel, and to make efforts after increasing her knowledge. I trust she is the subject of a change of heart."

"Tried today *(Monday)* to have some conversation with ——. I fear she knows but little of her own heart. Pastors in this land do not take so much for granted as do pastors in England. At least, I know very little was known of me when I was received into the Church.

"Our hearts were saddened this morning by hearing of the death of little ——, the only child of one of our most useful deacons. He and his wife are among the most regular and zealous Sabbath School teachers; and as Christians, have not only been consistent, but most exemplary. They are among the few upon whose moral charac-ter no stain has ever rested. Their dear little one was the object of their tenderest affection. I have often been delighted with the fond endearment manifested by Mrs. M—— to her babe. The black and colored people are not at all deficient in parental love, but are often rough in the manner of showing it. The speed with which the body decomposes is a great addition to the trial of bereavement. Twenty-four hours is the utmost that can be allowed for the beloved dead to remain above ground. In this case, not much more than twelve can have elapsed between death and interment. We sincerely sympathize with our dear friends, whose little one is now buried out of their sight."

Little did Mrs. H. think, when she recorded her sorrow for those bereaved parents, that before many months she would have to drink of the same cup, and know from painful experience the bitter pangs of a mother's grief, when called to part with her firstborn. That which she dreaded *did* come upon her; but when the time came, He who appointed the rod proved faithful to his promise—"As thy day so shall thy strength be."

CHAPTER 8

Parental Solicitude—Visit to a Sick Deacon—Anne's Last Visit to Chapel—Sickness and Death—Letter to her eldest Daughter—Teachers' Meetings—Sunday School Union—Christian Instruction and Dorcas Societies—Missionary Auxiliary—Death of a Fellow Laborer.

None but a mother placed in a similar situation—far away from beloved relatives and friends, without a neighbor to consult, constantly dreading imbecility in her firstborn—can imagine the intense anxiety Mrs. Henderson endured while watching over her child in its long continued unconsciousness. To such a mother, with her mind overburdened, bereavement under those circumstances would be thought a relief; and when the crisis came, the stroke was met with resignation to the divine will.

A few extracts from Mrs. Henderson's journal will serve to illustrate her state of mind preceding the death of Anne Eliza.

"Friday, 7th (February).—Have felt very poorly and excessively nervous all day. Last night, a little before ten, Anne awoke in a sad fright. . . . Despite every effort at composure, I could not be calm. One great calamity seemed ever staring me in the face—insanity for my poor child."

"Monday, 24th.—My poor Anne has had another of her bad frights. In some respects it was the worst I have witnessed. . . . I

asked myself, 'Is this my cross?' I fear it is. O that I may bear it with the same spirit as the Saviour bore the heavier cross for me!"

"*Thursday, 6th (March)*.—Went to B——, to see an old deacon of the Church who is laid aside. From his boyhood he has been a consistent follower of the Saviour.[1] When a boy, an aged Christian, since dead, used to take him to the private meetings of Christians, concealed under his coarse rough coat. To those meetings none but avowed Christians were admitted, lest enemies should betray them to the manager, who would be sure to punish them for such 'assembling of themselves together.'"

The child, often referred to in these pages, was very fond of the Sabbath School. It was a gratification to her parents to see her, morning and afternoon, walk cheerfully and take her place beside her classfellows. The last place little Anne visited with her mother was the house of God, on Friday evening, 12th September, at the last of a series of meetings held in Arundel Chapel, Buxton, with a view to promote a revival of religion in the Church and congregation. On the following Sabbath morning every member of the Mission family awoke early, and apparently in health; but the keen eye of a mother detected in Anne symptoms of indisposition. A fit came on, which was succeeded by fever, and on Tuesday morning the little sufferer gently fell asleep. O the value of revelation, in such a hour!

The following account of Anne's death was transmitted by her mother to her eldest daughter, then at Walthamstow:—

"Joan and Anne were delighted with their little letters. Anne showed hers to everyone about the house, saying it was from her 'big sister Charlotte.' I intended to have written to you for her, and

---

1 The person referred to has been many years one of the most zealous teachers in the Church, frequently undertaking long journeys, early and late, through all weathers, to carry the word of life to his fellow men. Even now he is active and useful.

to have guided her hand to sign it; but her dear little hand is now cold in death.

"On the evening of Friday, the 12th (September), she sat by my side in the house of God. On Sabbath, the 14th, when we awoke her to get dressed, she appeared sick. At seven, a.m., she had a fit. . . . On Monday morning she left her bed and went into the next room to kiss 'little Alice.' Fever soon came on again, and towards evening she began to suffer very much. On Tuesday morning we felt that she could not be with us very long: the fever would not yield. Her sufferings were now heartrending. Tossing to and fro, 'water,' 'water,' was the one thing she craved. At twelve o'clock, noon, on Tuesday, the 16th, our heavenly Father was pleased to release your little sister from her sufferings, at the early age of four years, to repose in the bosom of the Saviour. The following day she was interred in the same tomb with the ashes of your dear mother. We miss her very much—she was a universal favorite; but she is so much happier than we could ever have made her, that we rejoice on her account.

"My dear Charlotte, is not God speaking to *you* in this stroke? Had it been you, our tears would have been more bitter. We could not have felt much hope concerning you. You have never seen your dear sister: will you not meet her in heaven? Death, my dear child, may come to you as suddenly as it came to precious Anne. Oh, flee to the Saviour now, that it may be well with you!

"Dear Anne had been in the Sabbath School for some time. She loved her teacher and her class very much, and delighted to repeat many sweet hymns which she had learned. In the box I have sent you her hymn book and a lock of her hair. I have marked some of the hymns she learned and loved. Her sisters miss her very much: poor little Marianne has lost her playfellow, and is very lonely. The red beads I have sent you were picked from their pods by Anne and Marianne, who were delighted to send them to Charlotte. I hope you are really trying to improve your time now; let us have a good report respecting you. This will be a comfort to us in our sorrow, and lead us to thank God on your behalf."

It was the custom of the pastor's wife to invite the Sabbath School teachers, once a quarter, to tea, at the Mission House, Lusignan, for the purpose of affording an opportunity of more free, friendly, and profitable intercourse than could be had at other times. On these occasions she entered with all her heart into any proposal calculated to promote the prosperity of the Sabbath Schools.

Mrs. Henderson also took a deep interest in the East Coast Sunday School Union, and frequently read papers at the quarterly meetings. None entered upon any assigned subject with more cordiality than did she, when requested to prepare a paper upon "The best way of preparing lessons"—"Best means of instructing and impressing children"—"Best mode of teaching," etc. It was at these meetings that she first recommended to teachers many of those excellent helps in instruction which issue monthly from the British press—magazines for teachers and scholars, parents and children. At one of these, conversation turned on the propriety of canvassing for scholars in the surrounding villages. Few seemed disposed to attempt so new a thing, but one teacher brought eight new scholars the following Sabbath. Others were encouraged, and in a few months two teachers procured nearly a hundred new scholars.

The Christian Instruction Society also derived considerable assistance from Mrs. Henderson. She rendered essential service to her husband and fellow laborers by selecting suitable tracts, collecting facts and incidents calculated to encourage the tract distributors, besides making suggestions in harmony with the objects of the Society.

From the date of her arrival in Demerara, the poor old people in the congregation became objects of solicitude and care; and many of these were clothed with garments made by her own hands, assisted by some girls in the Day School. But the number of old people in destitute circumstances so increased, that she was unable to supply clothing. Many people in Demerara, how poor soever, are generous in giving food to their more destitute neighbors; indeed, many wretched and starving Coolies have been supported by the native laborers. To give money in such cases only supplied them with food; ready-made clothing for females could not be had. With a view to supply suitable garments, Mrs. Henderson formed a Dorcas Society; and although most of the females in the congregation were daily employed in agriculture, and could give but little assistance, she had the satisfaction of reporting at the end of the first year a considerable profit. Donations of prints, calico, etc., were occasionally sent by friends in England, through whose liberality many hearts "were made to sing for joy."

Indeed, whatever ministered to the temporal, mental, or spiritual good of young or old, afforded her pleasure. "I often think," she wrote, in referring to a supply of books for the schools, etc., "our resources in this way are like the widow's 'cruse of oil'—never very large, but never quite dried up. Thus does God incline our dear English friends to care for the people of this land. May we be faithful stewards of all entrusted to us; and may our people reap the benefit, and the donors a rich reward."

With her also originated the Buxton Auxiliary Missionary Society, in which she took a deep interest up to the week of her decease. She commenced with her own class, and the following year the Society included nearly all the adult and a goodly portion of the juvenile Sabbath Schools. She acted as secretary to the female branch, which was anything but a sinecure. With the hope of interesting parents and children, and as a guarantee that the subscriptions would reach their proper destination, Mrs. Henderson wrote herself, every month, upwards of 200 papers, containing the name of each subscriber, into which the subscriptions had been put, and "cast into the treasury." To encourage the spirit of self denial, and stimulate to reading, she also distributed monthly as many books, magazines, or tracts, with the subscriber's name written upon each.

An excellent Wesleyan catechist and schoolmaster, with his interesting family, resided in the village of ——, where he had been very useful and greatly esteemed. He was an amiable, industrious man, and also a faithful preacher. He had lingered several months, and arrived at the last stage of consumption. Being near, his afflicted partner generally called the Writer when critical symptoms appeared. A brief account of the peaceful death of that servant of Christ is here given, from Mrs. Henderson's journal.

"*Sabbath.*—Before my husband left the chapel this morning, a message came to say that Mr. M—— was much worse, and requested Mr. H. to go over and see him. I accompanied my husband; found Mrs. M—— greatly alarmed . . . The doctor had said he could not last long. Poor man! he clings most tenaciously to the hope of recovery. His large family presses heavily upon his spirit. In the event of his removal, they are entirely unprovided for. With a view to relieve Mrs. M—— a little, who is herself far from being well, I brought home William and Mary, who are already quite happy with our little ones."

"*Friday, 8 September.*—Soon after rising this morning, received the sad intelligence that Mr. M—— was no more. After hastily taking a little breakfast, we went over; found poor Mrs. M—— in great distress, but enabled to say, 'Blessed be the name of the Lord.' Remained until 10½, a.m.; then, seeing many friends around her, came home. Returned in the afternoon, and was with her until after the funeral. Thus a poor widow and five dear children are left destitute. They are the family of a *righteous man*, one who labored assiduously in the Lord's vineyard, and he will not allow them to want. Mr. B—— and my husband took part in the funeral. The people seemed much affected. I believe Mr. M—— was much beloved by many."

CHAPTER 9

*Various Results of Instruction—Extent of a Teacher's Influence—
Special Efforts for the Conversion of her Class—Hopeful Cases—
Penitent Backslider—Disappointed Hope—Efforts to induce the
Young to Read—Senior Bible Class—Buxton Sabbath School—
Total Abstinence.*

It is not a teacher's privilege always to see the immediate fruits
of his labors in conversions to God. There may be but few
instances of known conversions in a class; and yet, who will say
that the teacher's efforts are vain? Many have prayed and labored
for years, without being permitted to witness even one conversion;
but it would be contrary to experience to say that the life of such a
teacher had been utterly useless. "The work of spiritual reformation
is frequently like leaven in meal—progressing silently and steadily,
though imperceptibly."

This was true of the probable effects of Mrs. Henderson's exer-
tions among the young. Her usefulness should not be judged of
by the apparent number of conversions which are believed to have
taken place through her instrumentality (for such tokens of the
divine approbation were not withheld), but by her influence for
good over the minds and hearts of those under her instruction—
by the formation of character—by imparting a knowledge of the
truth, creating a taste for reading, and thus giving a hopeful bias

to their mental powers. Their improved domestic habits qualified them to fulfil the duties of life with comfort and satisfaction. Thus the influence of the faithful teacher may extend through a whole community, and tell beneficially on future generations after the toils of earth are ended; indeed, the beneficial results may be prolonged for many years.

Mrs. Henderson sought, by private interviews with those under her charge, to impress the thoughtless and to awaken the slumbering conscience, to induce decision in the wavering, and to reclaim the backslider and encourage the inquiring and the timid. Her journal records some of the means which she employed to save souls.

"Sabbath, 27 (April) . . . Found my class very attentive in the afternoon; yet I fear much good is not being done. There is a number of young women who have been year after year under instruction, and are still careless, hardened, and indifferent. I feel anxious to try the effect of *direct* faithful, affectionate appeals to them. For this purpose I have requested —— to come here on Saturday next. I wish to see only one at a time, to insure their coming and going home alone. O that they may be prepared to yield their hearts to God!"

"Saturday, 3 May.—Conversed with Mrs. ——, E. ——, Mrs. ——, and K. ——. Some improvement in the last. R——, whom I had asked to meet me, came. I was thankful to find her in a subdued and prepared state of mind. She was once a candidate for Church fellowship, but turned back. She says, Satan told her she would have more happiness and pleasure in the world than among God's people. She speaks of having been miserable ever since she turned from seeking the Saviour, and professes to be determined to give her heart to Christ at once. God grant that she may!"

"Saturday, 17.—Having requested F—— to come, had special conversation with her. She seemed to feel the appeals made to her, if tears may be looked upon as an indication of feeling. She has manifested the same before, but the effect has been transient; still there is

more hope than if she exhibited callousness. I must not lose sight of her; she has much to contend with in her natural temper.

"C—— evinced much feeling, particularly when the Saviour's love was spoken of, and the manner in which her backslidings had wounded him.

"C——, a girl out of my class, came to offer herself for Church fellowship. I hope she is not deceiving herself. I fear some of these girls are following in the track of their 'matters' (companions). Many of the people love company in everything. Hence they generally excuse themselves for their sins because 'plenty people do same.'"

"*Monday, 9th (June)*.—This afternoon, a youth once in the Day School, and for a long time past in my class in the Sabbath School, came to offer himself to the candidates' class. He has from his infancy been surrounded with the worst influences. Soon after he left the Day School, I feared he would turn out a reckless, bad youth; but when he continued at the Sabbath School, and his natural trickishness seemed to give way to a degree of gravity, I began to have some hopes respecting him. For the last three months I have watched him narrowly, and have been pleased with his growing seriousness. I trust that God has begun a good work in him."

"*Wednesday, 11th*.—Mrs. ——, a poor backslider, came. She does indeed seem to be drinking of the cup of trouble. I trust her expressed penitence is sincere, and not the sorrow of the world which worketh death—merely the consequences of her sufferings. Perhaps, up to the end of the year 18—, no persons in the married state lived in more happiness than did she and her husband. Now, how changed—both adulterers! I believe this is the consequence of a bad habit which too many husbands and wives have, of separating from each other for a time, for work, to visit friends, etc. In this case, the husband, who was much *dunned* for debt, had gone to his relatives at E—— to get work and some money. No provision was made for his wife; she was to work as usual, to support herself. He was absent seven months; saved forty dollars, with which he was about returning to the coast. Disappointed of his passage, he left his canister (a tin case, containing his clothes) in ——'s house. Here his money was taken out; but he did not miss it until after his return to ——. Would that this had been his only trouble! Scarcely at home, before he heard rumors of the unfaithfulness of his wife during his absence. The discovery of it seemed to make —— quite reckless. Counsels, admonitions, and prayers, were of no avail—for many months he wandered far from God; and although husband and wife passed through lengthened and severe affliction, that had not the effect of bringing him back to God. Exhortations and reproofs were blessed in bringing him to retrace his steps, and it is to be hoped both husband and wife are now penitent."

Of one in whom Mrs. Henderson took a deep interest from a child, a painful account is recorded.

"*Tuesday, 16th.*—Mr. H. went to town today quite suddenly and unexpectedly, by mid-day train, in the hope of bringing home to her parents a girl who eloped with a young man, a few days ago. I regret to say he did not accomplish his object any further than by discovering her place of concealment. This case has distressed us much; our disappointment has been great. When I came to this land, —— was a little girl in the Day School, distinguished from many by her open, laughing countenance, and apparent sincerity. Some time ago we began to entertain hopes of her piety. Our hopes seemed to receive confirmation, by her voluntarily coming and soliciting a place in the candidates' class. She was received with joy, and with more confidence than we usually put in the young. After she had been some time in the class, it was rumored that she was receiving and returning the addresses of an unprincipled young man. I saw her: she denied everything, *in toto*. I believed her. Charges were renewed: I saw her again. She admitted that the young man had proposed marriage, but protested that she had given him a refusal, unless he were changed. For the lie in the first interview she was excluded from the candidates' class, but continued her attendance in my Bible class, though she avoided all private intercourse with me. I several times asked her to remain after the service, to speak with me, but she never would."

"*Saturday, 11th (January, 185—)*. —— (the person referred to above) came, she said, to confess her sins. I had feared that she had become entirely reckless. Mr. H. and the office-bearers of the Sabbath School conversed with her a week ago, but whether this was the first step to her return I cannot say. She says she has wished to confess her sins a long time ago, and professes to be anxious about her soul. On these professions she will be permitted, with some others, to take her place in the Bible class for instruction. O that God may meet with her there! I must aim at her conversion."

The truth, thus directed to the heart of that young person, was blessed, it is hoped, for her conversion to God. She has been for some time a Church member, and is married to a pious young man.

Many more might have been added to these plain and unvarnished illustrations of Missionary work. There is no attempt to give a "color," by concealing what is discouraging, or giving only the "bright side." No sensible friend of Missions would desire such deception.

The subject of this memoir had a happy way of reaching the heart and conscience of the young. The Writer has known a few words from her accomplish more lasting good than hours of talking and lecturing by some others, equally well disposed and accomplished. She frequently sent individuals home to their closets with a barbed arrow in their hearts, who came to her in the spirit of the Pharisee. With great talkers she made short work of it; but to the tale of a humble penitent she would have listened for hours, if necessary.

Her good sense and sound judgment eminently qualified her for usefulness in the sphere which she occupied. Her counsel was frequently sought by old and young, especially by the "mothers in Israel," with whom she sympathized sincerely in their trials and difficulties. The young, also, reposed confidence in her judgment and affection, and frequently opened their minds more fully to her than to their own parents. Among inquirers and candidates for Christian fellowship, and in all cases of discipline among the female members of the Church, she proved an invaluable helper.

In prosecuting her work in the Day Schools she made everything bend to what was really useful. She never could be induced to teach unless she saw some profitable end was to be accomplished; not merely to gratify a certain taste, or for a vain display. She would not sacrifice the really useful for what only pleased or captivated.

Through her efforts, as already remarked, a library was formed for the Sabbath School, and many beneficial plans did she devise to interest the young people in the several books. It was chiefly through her efforts that upwards of 200 of the best English magazines were circulated every month in the Sabbath School at Buxton, in 1853. Most of these were paid in advance for the whole year, before the January parcel arrived in the colony. She was always studying to benefit the poor members of the Church, and engaged the cooperation of the young females in these efforts. Many were the means she employed to interest the young in Christian Missions, and not without success.

Had similar influences been exercised at their homes to those which Mrs. Henderson brought to bear upon the minds of the young in her class or in private, she might have rejoiced more frequently in witnessing individuals under her instruction consecrating themselves to God. But the lack of domestic training and discipline has been one of the great barriers throughout the West Indies to the diffusion of vital godliness. In a few instances the teacher's efforts were seconded by mothers who had themselves learned and felt the value of the gospel. The following is a brief account of the reception of one of Mrs. Henderson's class into the Church.

"*Sabbath.*—I have never witnessed more feeling than was exhibited this morning in the public recognition of —— as a member of

the Church. Her very youthful appearance gave her much interest
in the eyes of many, especially the mothers of young daughters. May
some of her classmates be brought to Christ!"

Since the opening of Arundel Chapel, Buxton, it has been cus-
tomary for parents and children to meet every Lord's-day morning
and afternoon for catechetical instruction, independently of public
worship morning and evening; and all ages may be seen there, from
the child of three years old to the man or woman of grey hairs,
arranged in classes according to their age and capacities. There, no
pupil supposes himself "too old" or "too big" to remain in a Bible
class, and consequently there never has been any difficulty in retain-
ing the scholars as they grew up to manhood and womanhood.
This, in part, accounts for the fact that Mrs. Henderson had in her
class many elder girls and young women. That is, however, only
one cause of the senior scholars in Buxton Sabbath School being
retained. Had these elder girls, or the youths in the other senior
Bible class, been obliged to listen to tame, vapid, and threadbare
stale preaching, they would soon have found stronger attractions
elsewhere. But their interest in the teaching increased with their
years. Sixteen years' experience has convinced the Writer that, of all
the means employed to benefit the African and Creole population
of Guiana, he has found none more efficient than a well conducted
Bible class; and no department of Missionary labor affords greater
satisfaction than the Sabbath Schools. In the midst of what is discouraging, the schools are his hope. They have raised up a band
of Sabbath School teachers who have been a great assistance, and
continue to be valuable coadjutors in the work of God. Sabbath
Schools, efficiently conducted, are valuable nurseries to the Church.
The additions made to the Church at Buxton, for several years, were
chiefly young people from the senior Bible classes.

It has long been the custom of the teachers to meet the pastor one evening every week, to study the lesson for the succeeding Sabbath. The same lesson is taught in the several classes, except

in the Infant School; the entire school is addressed afterward on some part of the lesson, by the pastor or a teacher; and each alternate lesson is illustrated by one of those Scripture prints published by Messrs. Varty and Co. The variety of subjects thus taught, and the uniformity observed throughout the school, add much to the advantage of the lessons and the addresses, which are generally listened to with marked attention.

Mrs. Henderson was no novice in Sabbath Schools. When she went to Guiana, she knew what it was to prepare thoroughly for her class, and what constituted an efficient teacher. Her opinion of teaching, after many years' experience in Demerara, may be gathered from the following extract from a letter to her youngest sister, which also contains a short account, of one of the half yearly meetings of the Sabbath Schools connected with the Demerara East Coast Sunday School Union. One of the objects of the Union was to bring the schools on the coast, with their teachers, together every half year, alternately at Beturnwagting and Buxton, when a sermon was preached to the children.

"Yesterday, being Easter Monday, our Sabbath School, with two others, assembled in Bethel Chapel, Beturnwagting Village, and listened attentively to a very excellent sermon preached by Mr. Rattray, from Psalm 34:11. After the children were dismissed, the ministers and teachers took lunch together. After lunch some speeches were made; and in the evening a public meeting was held, when several of the teachers delivered interesting addresses. At that meeting I was not present, having left at half past five.

"Tonight Mr. H. is showing the magic lantern, at Buxton, to the Sabbath School children and teachers. He dearly loves the Sabbath School, and is never more happy than when among the children.
"We hope the coming years will show that the labor bestowed upon our children has not been in vain. What are you doing, dear J——, in your part of the Saviour's vineyard? I hope you are a very regular, diligent, and faithful Sabbath School teacher. Let me hear about

your class when you next write. If you were here, we would give you a very large class of big girls; and, what is more, we would see that you *worked hard* to prepare your lessons for the Sabbath. All our teachers are under law: there is no such thing among us as every man doing what is 'right in his own eyes.' Mr. H. is never out of the Sabbath School a moment; indeed, he requests generally to take some class or other. I did not know what it was to *work* on Sabbath until I came here."

Although Mrs. Henderson was not a believer in the doctrines of total abstinence when in England, such was her conviction of the soundness of abstinence principles, that she became a total abstainer, as has been seen, on her arrival in Demerara, and continued so. Her views on this subject will, after eight years' experience and observation, be seen by an extract from a letter to her sister, occasioned by certain remarks of her sister's on a sermon preached in Surrey Chapel by the Rev. Albert Barnes, on a Sabbath evening in 1852:—

"And so, dear ——, you only think part of your Bible good enough to be explained on Sabbath. When would you permit the objectionable part, as you deem it, to be explained? You remind me of many of the black people, who, when anything is said of their domestic habits, their houses, or their lands, say, 'That no belong to you—you preach the gospel, and we shall hear you.' T—— sometimes advises such grumblers (ironically) to take Jehoiakim's plan, and cut out those portions of their Bibles that they do not approve of. Whatever you may think of teetotalism, it is a good thing."

Of the beneficial effects of total abstinence among the Writer's congregation, he cannot speak too highly. For thirteen years he has tried it, and found it conducive to his own health, comfort, and usefulness. No case of discipline from intemperance has occurred in the Church for years. The young have been well indoctrinated in the principles of temperance, and grow up with intelligent and sound views of the evil properties of alcoholic beverages. Many of them would as soon think of drinking prussic acid, as use alcohol in any form. Many of the young are members of the Band of Hope, and the "Band of Hope Review" is extensively circulated in the Sabbath Schools. Although several of the lads and youths in the senior Bible classes are daily surrounded with great inducements to drink rum diluted and sweetened, prepared frequently by individuals purposely to tempt them, the Writer has not known more than one instance, for several years, of these lads yielding to these baits. Temperance meetings are held at most of the stations in Guiana, and tracts are distributed. Societies have been formed in nearly every congregation, composed mostly of Church members; and the Writer is happy to add, all his brethren in the Mission are total abstainers.

CHAPTER 10

Departure of her Second Daughter for the Mission School—Ship Cressy—A Mother's Counsels and Prayers—Letter to her Daughter—Sermon to Schools—Family Instruction—The Absent Children—Visits Berbice—Mission Stations—Letters.

In common with most of the mothers laboring in the Mission field, Mrs. Henderson saw those early developments in her children which are common in tropical climates. This made her feel anxious to have her husband's second daughter, then ten years of age, removed from among the unfavorable influences, and to join her sister at the valuable institution for the education of Missionaries' daughters, at Walthamstow. An opportunity of carrying out her wishes presented itself in the spring of 1853, by the return of Mr. and Mrs. Hughes and their family to England.

On Saturday, the 26th April, the fine ship *Cressy* weighed anchor in the Demerara River, for London. The day before, Mr. and Mrs. Henderson accompanied their friends and fellow laborers "to the ship," where they parted with their beloved child. Many were the counsels which, for weeks previous, had been poured into the ears of that dear girl, about to leave the parental home for years; and many, too, were the fervent prayers, both with and for her, which were offered by her affectionate, fond, and faithful mother. With a view further to improve such a critical period in that child's life, the

anxious mother placed a letter into her daughter's hand, when taking leave of her—never, as it proved, to behold each other on earth
again; adding the request, that she would read it when alone:—

"MY DEAR DEAR JOAN: As I shall probably not have an opportunity of saying some things to you which I should like to do, I have
thought of writing them, while you are quietly sleeping.

"I have long felt, my dear child, a great anxiety respecting you.
That anxiety has been increasing daily, and it will still increase the
farther that you are removed from us. If I did not hope that your
removal to England would be for your good, I never would have
consented to it; but at the same time, I have many, many fears about
you.

"My fears arise from the fact that you carry about with you
an enemy, a 'deceitful heart,' which makes you call 'good evil, and
evil good'; and if that same enemy goes with you to England, and
obtains the mastery, you will profit little by the instructions of your
kind teachers and friends.

"Resolve, then, my dear Joan, to conquer this enemy. Ask God
to help you, and he will do it. You know where to find a true and
loving friend—the Saviour, who died that you might live.

"I need not say how anxiously we shall look for letters from
Walthamstow. What will your teachers' letters report about you?
You will need to strive very resolutely against indolence and your
temper. Let me beg of you, my dear girl, in all things to be straight-
forward. Let there be no concealment of anything. I will not say
more about these things, because I have so often spoken to you
about them.

"Be very kind to your companions; be generous. Avoid rudeness
of every kind. Be neat and orderly in your habits, and do not mind
if it costs you some trouble to be so: it will save time and trouble in
the end.

"I shall no longer point out your faults, for I shall not see them.
For a time they perhaps will be passed over, by those who do see

them, and these faults may grow stronger and stronger. Oh, my dear, dear child, I entreat you, believe that, unless your heart is changed, you will never, never be a happy child.

"My only comfort, my dear Joan, is in commending you to God—he is willing and waiting to bless you. Do not cast away the blessing, as Esau did.

"Farewell, my dear, dear child; farewell! May God's presence upon the sea cause you to consider your ways, and to turn to the Saviour.

"Pay the greatest attention to the advice of your kind teachers. We shall often speak of you, and I shall try and prevent your sisters from forgetting you, and shall teach dear baby to pronounce your name.

"God bless you, my dear girl!"

The letter from which the following extracts are taken, was sent by the first mail packet after the sailing of the *Cressy*:—

"When we left you, and took our seats in the small boat, we felt very sad; and when we returned to Mr. Wallbridge's, dear Marianne inquired very sorrowfully why we had left 'sister Joan in the ship?'

"We left the Brick Dam very early on Saturday morning, and the first thing we looked for was the *Cressy*. We soon descried her, with her sails filled, bounding majestically over the waters. We continued to see her at intervals along the coast, Marianne and Alice frequently standing on the seat of the waggon to get a glimpse of the 'nice ship.' . . . We had a splendid day (Easter Monday), and Mr. Williams (Wesleyan Missionary) preached a very nice sermon from Ecclesiastes 12:1 (to the Sabbath Schools). As dear papa wished to try and be present at the evening meeting, I packed a basket of provisions, etc. to enable us to remain at Beturnwagting all night. We invited all the officers of all the schools to dinner, and had a very pleasant day. In the afternoon we all took a walk in the village; and in the evening, after all the little ones were asleep, I went to the meeting . . . On Tuesday evening papa resumed the special services for the young, which were commenced just a year ago. I thought of you, dear Joan. You said, a year ago, you wished to serve God. You wept with others. What says your heart now?

"Since you left, Tom has got a pretty little tooth, and delights his sisters with his funny tricks. Last Sabbath afternoon papa commenced using the new Scripture prints at the time of the address. One will be used every alternate Sabbath. We hope to get the whole set soon. The moment the lamp is lighted every evening, Marianne and Alice ask for the pictures. They know almost everything about them, and are learning the hymns about Samuel, Daniel, and Gehazi, etc. We are sure to sing the 'child's desire' once or twice in the course of the evening . . . I hope, dear Joan, you will never forget the kindness of Mr. and Mrs. Hughes, but write to them after they go to Wales. When Alice says her prayers she always remembers to say, 'Take care of Joan upon the sea,' etc. I hope you have not omitted to pray for your anxious parents, and little sisters and brother. . . . May God bless you, my dear child, prays your affectionate,

"Mamma."

It will have been observed that Mrs. Henderson's solicitude for the best interests of her absent children was very great. Her counsels were characterized by good sense, cheerful seriousness, and strong affection; and when pointing out a fault, it was done with calmness and tenderness.

After expostulating with her eldest daughter on some points relative to conduct and study, she concludes thus:—

"Ponder this well, my dear Charlotte, and seek grace to turn unto the Lord. . . . I have been frequently poorly of late. Sometimes I think, dear Charlotte, that my work on earth may soon be done. Under any circumstances this may be looked forward to; but in a country like this at present, where disease is rife, and carrying off unexpectedly many daily, it becomes us to be prepared for the coming of the Bridegroom. I have had no serious illness, but often feel very unfit to go through my daily duties.

"*You* have, my dear child, much cause for gratitude. How graciously has God raised up kind friends to attend you when removed from us! I do hope you will *never, never* forget the trouble they have had on your account, and show, by your affection, diligence, and obedience, how grateful you feel. Your kind nurse and your dear schoolfellows have large additional claims upon your affection. Let none have to complain of you in this respect. Give our love to them all, and thank them for us, for their kindnesses to you.

. . . "We were pleased to see your last letter much better written than usual. Miss T———'s message, also, respecting your drawing, gratifies us. I hope you will become increasingly fond of this pleasant and useful art, and that your success in that may induce you to try and be equally successful in other branches of your education. . . . I hope, my dear Charlotte, you have been able to cast yourself upon the Saviour, for pardon and eternal life. Oh, my dear girl, do not trifle with the gracious invitations of the loving Saviour!"

When her family increased, it was seldom that Mrs. Henderson could be present at the evening service of the sanctuary; but, although generally fatigued by the long and almost continuous engagements of a tropical Sabbath, she uniformly devoted the evening to the instruction of her household. Her custom was to catechize all present, children and servants, who could remember anything of the sermon, or lessons which had been taught in the Sabbath School; and, in a simple, familiar, and interesting way, give a Bible lesson, which was generally illustrated by a picture. Her younger children were taught a suitable hymn; then came the usual domestic worship. In this way each of her children became familiar with Scripture characters and texts, and their minds were stored with infant hymns as soon as they could speak.

One Sabbath, one of her children, then seven years of age, had committed to memory the answer in the "Assembly's Catechism" to the question "What are the several benefits which do either accompany or flow from justification, adoption, and sanctification?" After having had it explained, the child turned and asked her mother the meaning of the word "assurance," in the answer, which she had forgotten. After receiving an explanation a second time, she appeared thoughtful, and turning again to her mother, said, "Mamma, do you feel sure that God loves you?" "Yes. If I did not, I should feel very unhappy." "Never," added that mother, "did I feel more the need of possessing a well founded hope of a personal interest in Christ, than at that moment."

For years Mr. and Mrs. Henderson had promised to pay a visit to their dear friends Mr. and Mrs. Dalgleish, and other members of the Berbice Mission; and on Wednesday, 13th April, 1853, they left George Town by the *Tyne* steamer for New Amsterdam, where they were most cordially received by the resident Missionary and his excellent wife. After visiting all the stations, except two, some distance up the Berbice River, and spending ten days of most interesting, refreshing, and profitable intercourse with his brethren, the Writer returned to Demerara on Saturday, and left his wife and children to spend a few days at the stations they had not visited. Domestic sickness caused a further delay for a week; and on the evening of 19th May they reached George Town, after a tedious passage from New Amsterdam. Mr. and Mrs. Henderson slept at the house of their esteemed friends Mr. and Mrs. Wallbridge, where they uniformly received the greatest kindness. Mrs. Henderson complained of indisposition, but felt somewhat better next day, and reached Lusignan in the afternoon.

In writing to her second daughter, while in Berbice, she gave a short and hurried account of that deeply interesting visit.

"We left Lusignan on the 12th instant, and spent the day and night at Mr. Wallbridge's. In the evening Mr. W. showed the magic lantern, after which they (children) supped together, and enjoyed themselves very much. The following morning, at eight o'clock, we went on board the steamer for Berbice. The day was peculiarly fine, but we all suffered from sea-sickness except Tom. We reached New Amsterdam about four, p.m. Mr. Dalgleish came on board for us. Mrs. Dalgleish feels Janey's death very much. Dear Marjory has had good health of late. She has just asked me to tell you that she can use her *right hand* much better than she could some time ago. I am quite delighted with her perfect submission and obedience to her dear mamma.

"All the Missionaries have been in to see us, and we hope soon to visit some of them in their own homes. The chapel here (New Amsterdam) is a beautiful building, far superior to any in Demerara. It has a fine organ. There is a large Sabbath School, juvenile and adult. I took a class on Sabbath morning and afternoon. Papa has preached several times here, and at the other Mission stations.

"On Monday we had a delightful boat trip up the Canje Creek, to Mr. Jansen's station. Mr. J. succeeded Mr. Heywood, when he left Berbice. He has nine children, most of them quite young. We were most kindly received. The station is the prettiest I have seen, having long walks of fruit trees. The children were delighted with everything.

"On Thursday, 21st, Mr. Bowrey took me and the children to his house at Rodborough, about ten miles from town, on the west coast of Berbice. The west coast of Berbice is a continuation of the east coast of Demerara, so that we might reach Mr. Bowrey's house from our own by land. Mr. and Mrs. Bowrey have three charming, well trained, obedient children. The house is nicely situated—not much bush, but savannah land opposite, where cattle graze. Mr. Bowrey has taken great pains to teach the (school) children to sing, on Curwen's system.

"While we were at Rodborough, Louisa had her birthday. She had a little tea party, which delighted all the little folks. We stayed a week at Rodborough, and then Mr. Bowrey took us to Ithaca, Mr. Roonie's station, about eleven miles distant. Ithaca is a village upon the Berbice River, exactly opposite town. We only spent one night at Ithaca. In the morning Mr. Dalgleish brought a boat to take us over to town.

"On the following Monday Mr. Pettigrew came to take us to his house, which is about twelve miles from town, on the east coast of Berbice. This is near the Corontyne River, about 48 miles from Surinam. Mr. Pettigrew has four children. We stayed there until today (May 6th). We have now one more station to visit, Lonsdale, where Mr. Foreman is . . . I have thought many times, dear Joan, how much you would have enjoyed this visit to Berbice. Your sisters have been very happy at every place we have visited. They have received much kindness from everyone.

"I long to hear from you, but I shall have to wait some weeks more. I hope you will soon be comfortably settled at Walthamstow. Be sure and write long letters. This letter is badly written; I have a bad pen. Am very weary. 'Hard-backs' (large beetles) are flying in great numbers in my face, upon the paper, etc., and preventing me from writing properly. But if I do not write under all these difficulties, this will be too late for the mail . . . I hope you will be very kind to all your dear companions. Be amiable to everyone. Remember, your young friends know much more than you do; do not therefore set up your judgment before theirs. Remember me very kindly to ———. Be a good girl; do what is right. Let us hear good accounts of you. May God bless you and your dear sister!"

CHAPTER 11

*Last Visit to the Sabbath School—Sickness—Parting Scene—
Message to her Class and Teachers—Happy State of Mind—Longs
to Depart—Last Farewell—Peaceful End—Funeral—Sermons by
Messrs. Rattray and Dalgleish.*

On Sabbath, 22nd May, Mrs. Henderson rose early, as usual, and accompanied her husband and family to chapel about eight o'clock. Many friends flocked around her to welcome her back, and make inquiries respecting her health and the children's. She took her class morning and afternoon, but felt considerably fatigued before the close of the afternoon's service. In the evening she remained at home with her children. When the Writer returned home after the evening service, he found his beloved wife resting on the sofa, and complaining of having taken cold. Before retiring to rest she conversed freely with her husband, and, among other things, spoke of the plan which Mr. and Mrs. D—— adopt of setting aside a part of their income for religious and benevolent purposes; and it was agreed to adopt the like practice. This was the last conversation she had with her husband in apparent health. Little did he think so, at the time!

On *Monday* morning Mrs. Henderson complained of nothing beyond a chilly and feverish feeling, supposed to be the effects of cold she had taken on her way from Berbice. The Writer had arranged to go from home that day, on business, but proposed to remain. Of this she would not hear, but urged him to go, and promised to send for a friend to be with her during his absence. Fever ensued during the day, which did not yield until next day. Unmistakable symptoms of that fell destroyer, yellow fever, made their appearance in the course of Tuesday evening, but this in no way alarmed her. She continued tranquil and cheerful, but became gradually weaker. From *Tuesday* afternoon, indeed, the Writer feared his beloved wife was about to be taken from him, and his heart sank within him as he marked the indications of approaching dissolution. He attempted several times, during the evening, to speak to her respecting her unconscious babe and their other children; but his heart failed, fearing an allusion to such a tender and trying subject, at such a crisis, might overpower her sinking frame. With a trembling heart and faltering voice, he said to her, on that Tuesday night, "You are very ill, dear." "Yes," she said, "I know I am." "Have you anything you wish to say?" he inquired. "Yes, dear, I wish you to send Marianne to Walthamstow, as soon as she is fit, and send Alice and Tommy to Mrs. D——till they are fit for Walthamstow." . . . "How long have you been thinking about these things?" "This evening." "And what made you think about all these things?" "Because I thought, when black vomit came on, it might end in death." "I hope you feel happy." "Peaceful, peaceful," she said; and added, "I have been an unprofitable servant, but my hope is in the finished work of the Lord Jesus Christ." "You know the foundation of God standeth sure, and you know *your* foundation is sure." "Yes," she said, "I have not that to seek." "You know that *that* blood which cleanseth from all sin is efficacious for you." "Yes, that's my only hope."

After a short pause, her husband again asked her if she had anything else to say. "Yes," she said; "tell father to make ready for following me. I hope my sisters are in the road to heaven. Tell Charlotte to be steadfast, and tell Joan to give her heart to Jesus." He asked if she would like to see her dear children. "Yes, as soon as I feel able." Stimulants revived her a little, and from that time she rallied considerably. Her children were brought in, and the dying mother kissed her babe, ten months old, and pressed him to her breast. She did the same to Alice, two years of age, and said, "Poor dears! they will not know anything of ever having a mother." To Alice she said, with the greatest calmness, "Alice will soon have no mamma. Mamma is going to Jesus." Marianne, four years of age, her third child, seemed awestruck. She gazed upon her dying mother with much apparent thoughtfulness. The affectionate and devoted parent kissed her alarmed child, and told her "she was going to Jesus, and charged her to be a good child, and to be kind to her little brother and sister." With the greatest composure she thus took leave of her helpless children, as if she had been only going on a short visit. Her husband asked, "Do you feel, dearest, that you can leave your dear babes in the hands of the blessed Redeemer?" "Yes," she said, "I believe that the God of the fatherless and the widow will not forsake the widower and his motherless children. They will miss me, poor dears! and you, love, will be a solitary wanderer." He said, "he often feared she would be left a lonely widow in the world, but never expected she would be taken first." "I never felt anxious," she said, "about that, love; but in *your* last sickness I tried to realize the possibility of a separation, but found it hard work to school my heart to it." "You will soon join dear Anne" (her firstborn). To which she replied, "Yes; she will know more than I do now."

When Mr. Simon, the catechist, came in, she affectionately took leave of him, and solemnly charged him to be faithful unto death; adding, "you have many opportunities of making known the Saviour." Turning to her husband, she said, "Charge my class to resist the truth no longer, but accept the Saviour. Warn them from the grave. Tell the teachers to labor to bring souls to Jesus." She then thanked her nurse and took leave of each of her servants, addressing to each suitable words of counsel. She appeared to be sinking fast, and all who saw her thought her end was near. After a little rest, she affectionately embraced her sorrowing husband, and spoke of the period they had been united in the closest and best of bonds as

having been "nine of the happiest years of her life." By means of stimulants she rallied again, which for a few minutes raised a faint hope
that she might yet be spared. She asked her husband to pray; he did
so, and read part of the 26th chapter of Isaiah, a portion of divine
truth which afforded her much comfort. She conversed freely, and
spoke much of the love of God as manifested in the gospel. For a
short time, the irritability of the stomach seemed subdued, but soon
returned with greater violence. In the afternoon of Wednesday one
of her medical attendants administered a soothing draught, after
which she slept for several hours; but about ten o'clock she became
worse, and apparently dying. She again took leave of her children
and husband, in the same calm and affectionate manner as she did
in the morning, took particular notice of every individual in the
room, and thanked several friends for their kindnesses to her, and
bade all "farewell." In reply to a question put by her husband, if she
felt happy now? she said, with much energy, "Peaceful." Some time
after, she asked what o'clock it was; and when told eleven, she said,
"at midnight the Bridegroom cometh." To all appearance her end
seemed to be near; but by means of stimulants she rallied once more.

On Thursday morning, the 26th, her very kind and beloved
friend, Mrs. Wallbridge, came with Mr. Wallbridge. In reply to her
question as to how she felt, Mrs. Henderson said, "Perfect peace."
During the morning she spoke of the character of God, as revealed
by Christ. At one time she remarked, "How wonderful! Our God
is a just God—and, the Saviour: strict in calling us to account—
and, the Saviour." She conversed freely with her dear friend and
her husband on the genius of the gospel, and when not speaking
appeared to be in deep meditation. At one time she looked up and
said, "Who shall separate us from the love of Christ?" etc. A heavenly smile brightening her countenance, she repeated with much
energy the beautiful lines—

"Jesus sought me when a stranger,
Wand'ring from the fold of God.

He, to rescue me from danger,
Interposed his precious blood.

"Oh, to grace how great a debtor
Daily I'm constrained to be!
Let that grace, Lord, like a fetter,
Bind my wand'ring heart to thee," etc.

As her pulse rose or fell, hope of her recovery revived or sunk; but from Tuesday night she neither expected nor desired to recover. After she had evidently engaged in silent prayer and meditation, her husband asked her "if she still felt happy?" To which the dying saint replied, "Yes, happy; perfect peace." He asked again, "if she felt Christ precious?" She said, with great firmness and energy, "Yes, precious."

About two, p.m., she became much weaker than in the early part of the morning. The Writer, who had watched her constantly day and night, from Tuesday afternoon, knew her end was now very near, and asked Mr. Wallbridge to come in and see his dying wife. He said to her, "You can say, He loved me and gave himself for me." "Yes," she said, "it is a faithful saying, and worthy of all acceptation, that Christ Jesus came into the world to save me, the chief of sinners." She asked him to pray with her, in which she joined fervently. From a calm and patient waiting for the coming of the Lord, her desire for that "better country" now increased to a strong wish to depart and be with Christ. In reply to a remark made by her husband, she said, "I know in whom I have believed, and am persuaded that he will keep that which I have committed to him against that day." She added, with much energy, "and now 'that day' has come." At another time she said, "I have fought a good fight, I have finished my course, I have kept the faith; henceforth there is laid up for me (I trust) a crown of righteousness, which the Lord, the righteous judge, shall give me at that day."

While her husband and friends were noticing every muscular

movement, expecting her end, the departing saint looked up with a heavenly smile and said, "I thought I had done with this world." One of her medical attendants having ordered a stimulant to be administered, she objected to take it, and said to her husband again—"Why keep me here?" Her breathing had become difficult and distressing, and she seemed to be dying. Contrary to the expectation of those present, she looked up again and spoke to her husband and children, embracing each with all the unabated affection of her loving heart. Looking her friend Mrs. Wallbridge in the face, she said, "This is slow work." After a severe muscular struggle, the faithful and devoted MISSIONARY'S WIFE fell asleep in Jesus, at six, p.m., on Thursday, 26th May, 1853, aged thirty-three years. "Blessed are the dead who die in the Lord."

What desolation and woe does death cause! What fearful havoc has sin produced in God's creation! Within that dwelling everything appears gloomy, deathlike! In a few hours, how changed were the sweet features of the beloved wife and affectionate mother, too plainly and painfully telling what disease had accomplished! Earth seemed tenfold more a dreary wilderness, and heaven alone was felt to be attractive, at that dread moment. There seemed to be little that was inviting within that dwelling. She, who was the center of affection and the mainspring of the enjoyments of that once happy family, lay cold in death. If sympathy caused tears to flow from the Son of God, who can deem it unmanly to weep when the heart is made to bleed beneath a blow like this?

Blessed be God for the never failing consolations of divine truth, and for the great and precious promises of his word, which afford the only true comfort to the believer when his spirit is, as it were, overwhelmed. The merciful and compassionate High Priest has not left his people "comfortless."

Swiftly did the sad tidings spread, far and wide. The pastor's house was soon filled with members of his congregation, who hastened to weep with him. It was of no avail urging them to return to their own homes that night, they would not leave "the house of mourning."

Early the next day many others hastened to take "the last look" of all that remained of their beloved teacher and friend. Many and bitter were the lamentations, for all felt that "a mother in Israel" had died. The sorrow and mourning were not confined to the Writer's congregation; many came from neighboring Churches to condole with the bereaved pastor and his orphan children.

In less than 24 hours, he who would have given up his life for her who had been thus suddenly torn from his embrace, was compelled to say, "bury my dead out of my sight." A most suitable address having been delivered to a large audience in Zion Chapel, and prayer offered by two brethren who knew how to minister consolation, devout men carried the MISSIONARY'S WIFE "to her burial, and made great lamentation over her."

Mr. Rattray, who remained at the Writer's residence, improved the event, in Arundel Chapel, Buxton, on the Sabbath, from 1st Corinthians 15:55. In the afternoon he addressed the Sabbath School, and delivered Mrs. Henderson's message to the teachers— "Labor to bring souls to Christ."

Next Lord's-day Mr. Dalgleish, of New Amsterdam, preached in the morning from Ecclesiastes 9:10, and in the evening from 1st Peter 5:6. On both occasions he improved the mysterious providence for the benefit of survivors. Would that the impressions made by the touching appeals to the hearts and consciences of the hearers may continue to result in the conversion of souls to God, in that congregation!

The loss occasioned by the decease of such a wife, and her removal as a fellow laborer in the Mission field, can be estimated by no one but those who daily witnessed her devotedness and enjoyed her society—who reaped the benefit of her cooperation, and now mourn the sad bereavement. A Christian lady, who had almost constant opportunities of witnessing Mrs. Henderson's everyday employment for upwards of nine years, said to the Writer, "I never met with another Miss Leslie!"

————————

The Writer earnestly prays that these and other incidents in Missionary life in the West Indies may excite more sympathy with and prayer for those who are occupied in that field of labor.

Few persons can comprehend the amount of injury which slavery inflicted upon the children of Ham residing in these West India colonies. Wholly to judge of the monstrosities of that accursed system, it is necessary to have mingled with those who continue to suffer from its debasements. Revolting as are the physical evils of slavery, they are not to be compared with the mental injuries the slave is doomed to suffer. Could British Christians but witness the evils which everywhere meet the Missionaries in those colonies—with the true character of the difficulties they have to encounter, besides their often proving insurmountable barriers to usefulness—British Christians would stand aghast.

It is not enough that Great Britain tardily meted out a portion of justice, and burst the fetters of the slave asunder, sixteen years ago; justice will not be satisfied till the African race in her colonies has full compensation for all the injuries inflicted upon it under the sanction of British laws—compensation made, not, certainly, by merely liberating the bones and sinews of the negro; nor by leaving him in a measure still unprotected, denying to him all the rights of a British subject, and moreover crushing him by oppressive taxation. If he were clothed in England's "broad cloth," placed in a palace, with Britain's gold lying at his feet, that could not compensate for the injury inflicted upon the man, nor retrieve the vigor of his mental faculties.

The Mission stations in the West Indies need still the lively sympathy, prayers, and fostering care of British Christians. It is not to be doubted but that the Churches and schools in Guiana—a land enriched with the dust of Smith and Wray, etc., and of honored women not a few—will be sustained with a liberality equal to their necessities, and far exceeding that which first gave to its enslaved inhabitants "the glorious gospel of the blessed God," nearly fifty years ago.

www.ingramcontent.com/pod-product-compliance
Lightning Source LLC
Chambersburg PA
CBHW031341040426

42443CB00006B/428